Outcome-Based Education

The State's Assault on Our Children's Values

by

Peg Luksik
and
Pamela Hobbs Hoffecker

HUNTINGTON HOUSE PUBLISHERS

Huntington House Publishers
P.O. Box 53788
Lafayette, Louisiana 70505

Library of Congress Card Catalog Number 94-78044
ISBN 1-56384-025-1

Printed in the U.S.A.

To our beloved husbands, because of the dishes they washed, the home-cooked dinners they missed, and the constant words of encouragement they offered—so we could write this book.

To our dear children. And to their children.

To our friend Susan Browne whose tireless editing and passion for grammar made our words sound literate.

To those OBE researchers around the nation, without whose help this book could not have been written. You know who you are, from Florida to Alaska, from Pennsylvania to Oregon. Thank you.

To Pam's father, Albert Hoyt Hobbs, who spent his career as a professor at University of Pennsylvania defending individuality and opposing social engineering. Although he died during the writing of this book, we pray that our voices will join his—speaking out for the protection of America's little ones.

CONTENTS

Chapter One   7

> What's OBE? The Bottom Line

Chapter Two   29

> Outrageous Outcomes

Chapter Three   55

> Mad, Mad, Mad Testing

Chapter Four   65

> The Marriage of Business and Education

Chapter Five   89

> How Do You Spell School? S-T-A-T-E

Chapter Six   111

> Brave New Family

Chapter Seven   137

          Touring an OBE Classroom

Chapter Eight   169

   Will the Real "Success" School Please Stand Up?

Chapter Nine   189

          What's a Person to Do?

Glossary   205

ONE

WHAT'S OBE? THE BOTTOM LINE

1984 teaches us the danger with which all men are confronted today, the danger of a society of automatons who will have lost every trace of individuality . . . yet who will not be aware of it.
— Eric Fromm, Afterword in *1984*

Pennsylvania. Birthplace of liberty, now mandates outcome-based education (OBE). It's parents day at an elementary school near beautiful Lake Erie. Seven-year-olds with scrubbed, smiling faces, each raise one arm with a tightly clenched fist, Black Panther-style. And, they start chanting:

> "We march shoulder to shoulder for children's rights."
> "No! No! We won't go!"
> "We won't do our chores."

At this upscale school, parents look at each other, stunned. "Nice way to knock parental authority!" Susy whispers. Her bewildered friend responds angrily, "What *is* outcome-based education?"[1]

That question is being asked from Alaska to Alabama, from Maine to Montana. If you haven't heard of OBE yet, you will—soon. Or, you will hear of one of its clones, Performance-Based Education (Pennsylvania, Washington), Outcome Driven Developmental Model (Arizona), Quality Performance Accreditation (Kansas), the Kentucky Education Reform Act, Re-Learning (Arkansas), Common Core of Learning (Virginia, Connecticut).

7

Although it's as quiet as a termite, OBE is coming—it's in your state right now. If not stopped, some form of outcome-based education will be mandated across America—in all fifty states.

Oregon. Land of rugged freethinkers and OBE. High schoolers are completing a Values Appraisal for their Wellness and Me Portfolio. Instructions say, "This tool will enable you to remain focused on your . . . well-being, as well as to achieve the . . . outcomes." A few students tap their pencils nervously wondering, in a public school where God has been banned, how should they respond—on a scale of 0–10—to one hundred statements such as:

#34. I believe that tithing (giving 1/10 of one's earnings to the church) is one's duty to God.

#11. I have a close relationship with either my father or mother.

#91. If I ask God for forgiveness, my sins are forgiven.[2]

Students internalize, "Will I be considered 'well' if I love my parents and believe in a living God?"

The same test pops up in eleventh-grade English classes in Connecticut; and, another in seventh grade in North Carolina. Why are OBE schools appraising students' values, without parental knowledge or consent?

Colorado. A principal at one of OBE's national showcase schools refuses to agree that every graduate should know something about the Holocaust. He explained, "A curriculum that includes specific facts is outdated in a changing world."[3] Does OBE discourage learning facts?

Oklahoma. A teacher complains, "Children are not learning grammar at all. Tests can be taken over and over and over. We are not allowed, in our [OBE] school, to give anything below an *A* or a *B*."[4] Why does OBE discourage competition?

Charting the Difference

Outcome-based education (OBE) differs from traditional education in both structure and content. In a nutshell, here are a few differences:

Traditional Education (ABCs)	Outcome-Based Education (OBE)
Grade Level/Standards of Learning	
Specific grade levels K-12. Each grade level has distinct subject content that each student is expected to have learned at the end of each grade.	No specific grade levels (multiage groups). Intermittent benchmarks gauge progress toward mastering learner outcomes.
Graduation Requirements	
Students must pass specifically defined academic courses, earning Carnegie Units toward a high school diploma.	Students master specific learner outcomes, which include nonacademic, subjective attitudes to earn a certificate of mastery.
Focus of Teaching	
Academic in nature. Emphasis on content of academic material (what the student knows).	Affective in nature. Emphasis on application of skills and knowledge (how the student uses information).
Method of Teaching	
Information taught in specific courses (math, history, English, etc.), which each student is responsible for learning over a specific time frame (one school year).	Information in broad themes, taught across the curriculum (interdisciplinary). Individuals learn within groups or using individual education plans (IEP).
Time is constant. Content varies.	Time varies. Outcomes are constant.
Teacher models, but does not grade, traditional values and attitudes. Knowledge of facts and comprehension assessed.	Teacher assesses behavior, values, and attitudes— self- esteem, coping skills, compromise skills, proper citizenship attitudes for an interdependent, global society ("higher order thinking skills").

Teacher is instructor, leader. Reading books is emphasized. Textbooks supplement content-rich curriculum. Students receive guidance and instruction.

Teacher is "coach"; facilitator. Computer learning is emphasized (reading is "passive"). Textbooks are discarded. Students are self-directed learners.

Grouping

Students are often grouped according to achievement levels and needs (honors, remedial, etc.).

No grouping by ability. Faster or older students tutor slower or younger pupils.

Grading Scale

A, B, C, D, F—grades reward each student according to his/her achievement level. Students are responsible for earning passing grades in order to advance.

A, B, I (Incomplete)— no one receives a C or below. Students are remediated until achieving "mastery" of a learner outcome. No one fails.

Testing

Stanford Achievement Test, Iowa Test (objective assessments of student achievement and aptitude).

Portfolios, projects, assessment tests determine how students demonstrate "mastery" of learner outcomes (includes subjective teacher assessment of attitudes, values, etc.).

Schools

Schools are part of the community.

Community is part of the schools.

War is raging in the classroom. It involves America's new education reform: Outcome-Based Education (OBE) vs. Traditional Education (ABCs). Not limited to the school building, OBE will intrude into your family, into your community. It's a battle over who will control America's children.

To OBE or Not to OBE?

Proponents applaud outcome-based education. In fact, OBE enthusiasts often use the language of the born-again convert. "To believers, outcome-based education (OBE) is a silver bullet with dramatic potential for changing American schools," brag education writers Jean King and Karen Evans.[5] Outcome-based education is touted as a "world-class" education that will prepare students to compete in the twenty-first century's global economy. Business is crying out for well-prepared workers. And, since the "Norman Rockwell" family no longer exists, OBE schools must step in to form parent/school partnerships.

"Your 'silver bullets' are academic blanks," respond disillusioned opponents. They contend there's no valid research proving that OBE works. Grassroots organizations checked many "successful pilot programs" and found the same pattern—higher spending, lower achievement. Littleton, Colorado, to mention one, spent more than 1.3 million dollars, didn't like OBE's watered-down academics, and dumped it.

Former U.S. Secretary of Education William J. Bennett doesn't mince words. He calls OBE a "Trojan Horse"—rolling into elementary and secondary schools—filled with "politically correct" thinking. But, even more serious, according to Bennett, "OBE can be used to undermine parental authority and traditional moral beliefs."[6]

Both sides, however, agree on one point: America's schools need help. Studies show that nearly one-half of American seventeen-year-olds do not know who Joseph Stalin was.[7] And, since 1970, SATs plunged about sixty points—except for a random group of high schools. Although schools where SAT scores remained strong had little in common (some located in posh suburbs, others in blue-collar inner cities), they shared one secret. According to *Guidelines for Improving SAT Scores*, their secret was a dogged commitment to stressing grammar, vocabulary, and ability grouping.[8]

Reform is necessary, but will outcome-based education help students leave high school knowing Stalin was responsible for more deaths than Hitler? The word *reform* means to make changes for the better or to return to a former good state. Restructuring or transformation means simply to change—not necessarily for the better. Is OBE's reform/restructuring change for change's sake?[9] Or, will it give our ailing schools a much-needed megadose of historical facts and traditional content?

Let's see about facts. Fifteen-year-old Tim bursts in the kitchen door, plunks down his backpack on the wooden table, and announces, "My history-English teacher told my class he wasn't supposed to teach us facts anymore, only 'problem solving' and 'critical thinking.' " Tim's mother rolls her eyes. "Will 'problem solving' teach my son the fact that Abe Lincoln wrote the Emancipation Proclamation?" Tim's OBE high school's shift away from teaching facts is consistent with OBE dogma. A promotional article, "It's Time to Take a Close Look at Outcome-Based Education," clearly states, "Factual recall fade[s] into the background."[10]

What about teaching reading, writing, and arithmetic? State Superintendent of Schools and outcome-based promoter Sandy Garrett proudly writes in Oklahoma's *Learner Outcomes* that OBE is "not a 'back to basics' approach."[11]

Defining OBE

Concerned citizens across our land—moms and dads, legislators and administrators, taxpayers and teachers—demand, "If outcome-based education is not about teaching facts or the three Rs, what is it?"

Simply put, its intent is to change American education, totally. It's national, it's radical. Marc Tucker, president of the pro-OBE National Center on Education and the Economy explains, "You can't really break the mold [of America's schools] without changing the whole system all at once—every piece of it."[12]

Maybe that's a good idea. But, only if you replace it with something better. Imagine a sledge hammer smashing a plaster-of-Paris mold of the traditional school. The hammer pounds away until nothing you'd recognize as "school" is left. No final exams, no valedictorian, no graduation diploma, no spelling bees, not even a school building used solely for education. Now the psychologist/sociologist/educators pour all American schools into their OBE mold. They've created a *totally* new American school.

That's an accurate way to define OBE—it completely breaks the traditional education mold.

OBE's new mold totally changes requirements for high school graduation, by eliminating the Carnegie Units (four units of English, three units of math, etc.). In traditional education, the student successfully completed required units (usually twenty-one) then graduated. Papers, tests, and final exams gauged what a student knew and could do at any point. In contrast, time spent taking courses now is irrelevant. OBE mandates that a student must demonstrate "mastery" of every outcome (specific goals defined by the state) in order to graduate.

As you know, outcomes aren't new. They're nothing more than learning goals. For instance, an outcome in geometry might be understanding that two parallel lines don't meet. Students demonstrate they've grasped that axiom by completing problems. The answer is clearly right or wrong.

In contrast, many OBE outcomes involve personality, attitudes, and behaviors. And, the state is holding the yardstick. Measuring up to government standards will determine if your child will graduate. Look at some typical outcomes. These are Arkansas' outcomes:[13]

- Exhibit personal adaptability to change.
- Accept the responsibility for preserving the earth for future generations.
- Realistically assess personal strengths and weaknesses.
- Appreciate racial, ethnic, religious, and political differences.
- Function effectively in a multicultural environment.
- Exhibit positive self-concept and a sense of self-worth.

Will your child "accept the responsibility for preserving the earth for future generations" if she doesn't believe in birth control or abortion? And, why teach students to embrace "personal adaptability to change"? In 1938, patriotic Germans resisted change, while others adapted to Hitler's "new Germany." How do you grade a child in "appreciating racial, ethnic, religious, and political systems"? A youngster should be taught about political differences. But, should every political system, including Marxism, be "appreciated"? Should religions such as Wicca be "appreciated"? People—not ideologies—should be "appreciated."

Across America, states are quietly passing legislation changing graduation requirements. Beginning in 1996, Minnesota ninth-graders won't work toward a diploma based on how many hours of social studies or math they've completed. Instead, they will be expected to meet outcomes.

How will "mastery" of outcomes be evaluated? According to Alabama's OBE blueprint, "Nationally-normed standardized test should be phased out."[14] OBE's new graduation criteria requires passing high-stakes assessment tests tied to the outcomes, which entail subjective evaluations. (Details in chapter 3, "Mad, Mad, Mad Testing.") As if that weren't enough, a new "universally" recognized certificate, called the Certificate of Initial Mastery (CIM),[15] will eventually supersede the antiquated high-school diploma.[16]

Significantly, instead of the state mandating that the school must provide specific Carnegie Units of academic input, now the state mandates that the individual child must know and do specific outcomes.

In other words, high schools will withhold this new CIM certificate until your child gets every outcome right—no matter how long that takes. In the OBE-ish state of Kentucky, a law mandates that "additional time to achieve the outcomes . . . may include extended days, extended weeks, or extended years."[17]

This gives new meaning to OBE/restructuring's familiar term, *lifelong learning*, particularly when one remembers that every child must meet every outcome to graduate. What's the fuss? Children always have had to pass courses in order to complete high school. But, with OBE, some parents may discourage their children from attaining certain nonacademic outcomes. For example, in a Riceville, Iowa, sophomore English class, attitudes about population responsibility and voluntary poverty were assessed in a "Simplicity Survey." Look at two sample situations:

> "I and my family will have no more than two children."

> "I and my family will own no more than three sets of clothes per person."

This survey shows how outcome-based education works. If you as a student don't score high in the "committed" level, the test says a "teacher may ask you to retake this survey in order to see if the unit changes your commitment." That's what outcome-based education is about. Retaking tests, with no penalty, until you "get" the right attitude (outcome).

Obviously, schools have always taught goals or outcomes. That's as old as education. But, mandating so many nonacademic outcomes is new. Parents who fear outcomes such as ecology, wellness, and understanding diversity may become political minefields. In other words, will your child be tested and retested about how he will "solve" the perceived overpopulation problem? (Details in chapter 2, "Outrageous Outcomes.")

OBE clearly states that it must break the mold of traditional education. However, this mammoth reform is much broader than simply devaluating facts and the three Rs, mandating questionable outcomes, or even changing graduation requirements.

Defining a Shadow

Because it breaks the mold of American education, trying to explain education restructuring is like putting a shadow in a box. OBE moves, it changes, it grows, it takes on different shapes. It evolves through phases. OBE advocates use double-entendre expressions. They say things such as "new basics" but mean outcomes such as "cooperating

with others." After reading several major education journals, a confused *L.A. Times* columnist asked, "What exactly
is outcome-based education, if anything?" He decided the
term defies definition.[18] Dr. Thomas Sowell, author of *Inside American Education*, equally as frustrated, says outcome-
based education "means nothing like what it seems to
mean."[19]

Is this reform's definition of intentionally vague? Many
say yes. If you oppose this reform in your school district,
but can't tell people what it is, how can you stop OBE? Try
mortally wounding a shadow.

Even its chief promoter, Dr. William Spady, admits,
"The real meaning of the term outcome-based is far different from the way most people think of it."[20]

OBE = Outcome-Based Egalitarianism

While its label is relatively new, OBE actually was developed over several decades. Dr. William Spady, a sociologist
and director of the International Center on Outcome-Based
Education, coined its name. He's a highly paid OBE consultant who has visited almost every state. Spady believes
the traditional American school is a relic of the industrial
age and therefore must be transformed, totally.

You might say his theme is "school's out, OBE's in"
when he writes, "The authentic meaning of the term [out-
come-based] has tremendous implications for the complete
transformation of our educational system."[21] One way he
begins transforming schools is by making "competition" a
dirty word. He proposes:

- getting rid of the bell curve

- phasing out averaging systems (QPAs) and com-
parative grading (report cards with any grades lower
than a *B*)

- making instructional methods and materials used
in gifted programs accessible to all students (no more
"elitist" gifted programs)

- phasing out factual recall (end memorizing historical facts, vocabulary lists, multiplication tables, spelling lists)[22]

OBE throws one hundred years of traditional three Rs education—with its textbooks, grades, standardized tests, diplomas—out America's schoolroom windows. Ability-grouping in reading and math disappears. Papers can be resubmitted and tests retaken, without penalty. Almost anything that smacks of competition goes, eventually.

That's why Kentucky, which passed its performance-based (OBE-style) law in 1990, wanted to cancel its traditional, statewide spelling bee. According to Kentucky's teachers union, "The event's emphasis on rote memorization and competition contradicted the spirit of the state's [outcome-based] school reform law."[23]

Report cards in Kentucky's primary schools dropped traditional letter grades to use, for example: *M*, "Most of the time"; *S*, "Some of the time"; and *NY*, "Not Yet."[24]

Many school teachers question OBE. "There's competition in life," Robert Murphy, a concerned middle school teacher, told Kentucky's *Lexington Herald-Leader*. "If we're not showing children there's competition in school, when we throw them out into the world they're going to have a rude awakening."[25]

Although OBE packages itself as an education that prepares students to be workers for the twenty-first century, every outcome-based education promoter whistles the same anti-competition tune, "All students shall succeed." Sounds wonderful—until you realize that Jane (I.Q. of 140) and Billy (I.Q. of 90) must both master the same outcomes successfully.

It's egalitarian, not academic. The only two ways all children will succeed are: 1) eliminate failure; 2) inflate grades.

Yet, in his pro-OBE article, "Fourteen Principles of Quality OBE," Albert Mamary writes, "Outcome-based schools believe there should be no failure." Restructuring enthusiast Alan November adds, "All students should achieve at least a 'B' in every subject."[26]

Michigan's Bay City public schools created "success for

all" by eliminating failure and inflating grades. "There was excitement the first year. Then reality set in," remembers Dave Johnson, then dean of students. When they adopted OBE, the district outlawed any grade lower than a *B*. Their outcome-based model allowed students to retake tests until earning an *A* or *B* or *I* (*Incomplete*). No one failed. But many students lost, academically.

"Grades meant nothing," says Johnson. The number of "incompletes" one year skyrocketed to three thousand. Counsellors had no way of sorting students so they could really learn. Some pupils weren't ready for geometry, although their record showed they received a *B* in algebra. But, they had not grasped problem solving; they just knew how to take the test. "Some youngsters re-took tests fourteen times," he said. OBE allowed kids to be irresponsible. Top students felt cheated. They studied hard to earn good grades while most of their friends watched movies the night before tests knowing they would be eventually getting the same *A* or *B*. After three years Bay City schools dumped outcome-based education and reintroduced an *A-F* grading system.[27]

OBE is like an academic track meet where the high jump comes with world class standards but no crossbar, because hitting it could hurt self-esteem. Dr. Spady firmly insists, "We need to fundamentally revisit the notion of competition."[28]

Revisit the notion of competition? America's capitalistic society successfully thrives on competition. Historically, socialist countries like China suppressed competition, while in America's economy, competing is strongly encouraged. After all, it's the heart of capitalism.

OBE's Crystal Ball

What's the light guiding OBE? Futurism. Its gurus say, "OBE's guiding vision of the graduate is that of a competent future citizen."[29] Strategic planning uses future-scanning procedures to determine exit outcomes. Spady himself wrote "Assumptions Regarding the Future," in which he predicted, "Despite the historical trend toward intellectual enlightenment ... there has been a major rise in religious ... orthodoxy ... fundamentalism and conservatism with which *young people will have to be prepared to deal*" (emphasis added).[30]

Is Spady suggesting fundamentalism and conservatism are anti-intellectual? Should schools spend time designing outcomes to prepare young people to deal with individuals who embrace religious, orthodox, or conservative viewpoints? In the future will conservative thinking become dangerous? Does this sound like "politically correct" bigotry?

In 1930, German anti-Semitic futurists predicted that Jews would destroy the world. Dr. Sylvia Kramer, who holds a history Ph.D. from Johns Hopkins, points out that pre-war German schools used innocent-looking genealogy surveys to collect information for Hitler's "final solution." In 1992, an Iowa school took the following survey, without parental knowledge or consent. High schoolers were given a listing of fifteen nationalities and religions such as "1) Irish-American, 2) Hispanic-American ... , 9) German-Americans ... , 16) Jews, 17) Catholics, 18) Protestants." Students obediently followed instructions, "Please answer as honestly as you can."

> Which of the above do you think would be most likely to eliminate an entire race?
>
> If you could eliminate an entire race would you?
>
> If yes, which one?[31]

What has happened to the public school mission to develop each student to his academic potential? Who started this idea to change attitudes through outcomes?

OBE's Roots

Actually, OBE is a psychologist/educator's new label to sell two battered theories: B. F. Skinner's operant conditioning (assess, teach, reassess, re-teach, etc.) based on his premise that all can learn, but not on the same day, and

Benjamin Bloom's theories from his book *Taxonomy*,[32] which added the "affective domain" (feelings, beliefs, attitudes).

Education Week credited Skinner with developing Mastery Learning[33] (OBE's previous name). Dr. Spady confirms that OBE is based on the theories of Professor Benjamin Bloom.[34] Today, Bloom's *Taxonomy* so strongly influences OBE programs that Northville, Michigan, public schools use a report card that grades students in the category, "Understands Bloom's *Taxonomy*."[35] To grasp OBE, one should know Bloom's definitions of 1) good teaching, and 2) the school's purpose.

Bloom defines " 'good teaching' as a teacher's ability to . . . challenge the students' fixed beliefs."[36] What? Don't parents carefully try to "fix" belief in morals, in God, in family, before sending their little ones to school? Yet, across the country teachers are using a "Developing Nurturing Skills" curriculum, which tells fifth-graders, "You are expected to keep confidential anything that is discussed in the classroom." Then, children are given a handout called, "MY BELIEF—MY PARENTS' BELIEFS." Fifth graders dutifully fill in blanks for questions such as: "Women should stay home to raise their children. My belief: _____. My parents' belief: _____." And, "Religion should be an important part of everyone's life. My belief: _____. My parents' belief: _____." Parents send little ones to school so they will learn 2 plus 2 and C-A-T, not to have family beliefs challenged.

Isn't learning the purpose of school? Bloom responds, "The purpose of . . . the schools is to *change the thoughts, feelings and actions of students*" (emphasis added).[37] Essential to OBEs restructuring is changing attitudes (feelings) and actions (behaviors). How does OBE implement this theory in the classroom?

Deborah is discovering how OBE will change her child's thoughts, feelings, and actions. She stares at the overhead transparency's words projected on a screen, "KNOW-DO-BE LIKE." The school superintendent explains to Deborah and the other parents, "The key to OBE is focusing on what students should *know, do* and *be like*."[38] Deborah bristles. "Sure, students should 'know' material. You learn ideas. But '*do*' and '*be like*'?" Since the next transparency says, "ORIENTATIONS [*be like*] = ATTITUDES," should her daughter be like someone who hugs trees or cuts trees down? The correct attitude for this Ohio schools outcome is "make decisions that conserve the natural environment."[39]

Once a proper attitude toward Ohio's outcome of "making decisions that conserve the natural environment" is taught, then children must do it. One kindergarten class spent school time picking up litter on a busy highway.

Even citizens who see no dangers in changing attitudes and beliefs demand to know, what is the bottom line, academically?

The Spady Bunch

Was Benjamin Bloom's Mastery Learning (ML) successful? Spady told *Education Leadership* that, in 1980, he and a group of experts convened to form the Network for Outcome-Based Schools: "Most of the people who were there . . . had a strong background in Mastery Learning, since it was what OBE was called at the time. But I pleaded with the group not to use the name 'mastery learning' in the network's new name because the word 'mastery' had already been destroyed through poor implementation."[40]

What does he mean by "poor implementation"? Ask parents in Chicago's five hundred public schools. Although their Mastery Learning was heralded as a "pacesetter for the nation" and mandated for half a decade in Chicago, standardized reading scores fell dramatically during its use. According to many Chicago public school teachers, students "were entering high school having successfully completed the ML [Mastery Learning] program without ever having read a book and without being able to read one."[41] By 1981, frustrated black parents demanded ML/OBE be ousted and filed a lawsuit for "educational malpractice."[42]

OBE/ML is academically unsound. And, philosophically it debunks the traditional idea of knowledge for knowledge's sake, replacing it with education for the sake of "real life" situations. Why? To prepare children for the workforce (see chapter 4). Rather than education serving the child, now the child is groomed to serve society.

Federal Connection

Education's paradigm shift, or new model, is no accident. For more than a decade, performance-based education (OBE) was quietly dropped into local districts through grant money—by the U.S. government. In 1984, the Far West Laboratory for Education (its director was Dr. Spady) applied for a federal grant. Spady's lab received a grant of more than six hundred thousand dollars to "put outcome-based education in place . . . in all schools of the nation."[43]

This grant includes outcome-based education elements now familiar to many opponents of OBE/restructuring such as:

- one-track system (eliminating the general track)
- multiage grouping (including ungraded primary)
- longer blocks of class time
- longer school year
- peer tutoring
- teacher certification modification
- technologies
- school/business partnerships
- site-based advisory councils
- children beginning school at age four

Its proposal spotlights three schools for their "commitment" to OBE principles.[44] In fact, one of them, Center School, in New Canaan, Connecticut, continued to be loudly touted as a national model of OBE by Dr. Spady and various departments of education until 1993. That year citizens discovered Center School had been closed for a decade[45]—it's now a parking lot. And, a 1987 government report stated that none of the grant's three schools were " 'exemplary schools' deserving emulation."[46] (Interestingly, today only one of those three "committed" schools still uses OBE.[47])

Spady's grant proposal frequently quotes OBE theorists Mortimer Adler, Ernest Boyer, John Goodlad, and Theodore Sizer. Sizer's Coalition of Essential Schools (CES) promotes his form of OBE, called Re-learning (now used in seventeen states). In 1970, Sizer wrote that teachers' "sermonizing" about "right" and "wrong" denies individual autonomy, which "lies at the heart of a new morality."[48] What is the school's "new morality"—moral relativism? And, the next year, John Goodlad published a report stating that most youth "still hold the same values as their parents . . . and if we do not re-socialize . . . , our system may decay."[49]

Outcome-based education is our government's "Play Doh" molding machine for resocializing school children. The state's human resources—your children—must *know*, *do*, and *be like* skilled, cooperative workers—not philosophers, historians or poets.

National Education "Care Plan"

Hillary Rodham Clinton and Ira Magaziner, the same duo who created President Clinton's socialized health care package, are also behind-the-scene architects of OBE's career-oriented education. They coauthored an article in *Educational Leadership* mapping out how to wed high schools to the workplace. It's a giant step toward socialized education. They wrote about nationalizing standards. Two of their recommendations include 1) "nationally established performance-based standards" that "should be set for all students," and 2) nationally established assessments standard (national test?) students must pass to achieve the Certificate of Initial Mastery (CIM).[50] OBE's new "diploma" will be the CIM. Oregon already mandates the CIM and uses it to certify that students have mastered state outcomes. This CIM is a theme of the U.S. Department of Labor manual called the *SCANS* report. Relying heavily on Clinton's and Magaziner's ideas, the Department of Labor (you read that correctly, "Labor" not "Education") is telling schools how to go about "Reinventing K-12."[51]

Why is outcome-based education necessary to this reinvention of American education? OBE is a system geared toward efficiently changing attitudes and behavior skills. Although it may create a compliant workforce, will it produce inventors?

Historically, ethics and attitudes were the sacred domain of houses of worship and families. Now, values, skills, and attitudes—called outcomes—must be taught, evaluated, then remediated to make children into well-oiled, compliant workers.

Elitists promoting OBE are restructuring schools to churn out quotas of semiliterate workers. Students will be trained to perform menial tasks under supervision in order to serve the demands of the global economy. Syndicated columnist and education watchdog Phyllis Schlafly sadly quips, "OBE is converting the three R's to the three D's: Deliberately Dumbed Down."[52]

How will OBE affect the community? The family? Remember Susy (mentioned in the beginning of this chapter) who watched her second grader's we-won't-do-our-chores presentation? Well, immediately after that evening, Susy dived into researching OBE.

Before long she discovered a handout from Ohio's Department of Education.[53] It showed a side-by-side comparison of traditional education—renamed (sarcastically) the "Norman Rockwell School," vs. outcome-based education—christened (patriotically) the "New American School." Like a page out of George Orwell's *1984*, the outcome-based column showed what all American schools would soon look like: promotion based on outcomes; teacher as mentor/coach/facilitator; individualized instruction plans using technology; multiple intelligences; collaborative learning; and reading considered "passive" learning.

It continued: open all year long, seven days a week (including the Sabbath), offering on-site social services (including school-based clinics), computerized, detailed records of each learner (sounds like Big Brother). Susy realized the school, a government building, would become the center of every community.

Suddenly, the words "learning-cohort families" leaped

off the page at Susy. Family? Was the government school redefining itself as "family"? Recently, she had read about a school in North Carolina whose restructuring is based on the philosophy, "Norman Rockwell is dead." It explained, "The traditional average American family doesn't exist."[54]

Today, Susy is one of America's many activists opposing OBE. If you ask her, "What's OBE?" she'll tell you that it:

- assumes the family is dysfunctional, and therefore undermines parental authority
- shifts education's focus from the three Rs to "real life learning"
- eliminates competition
- uses cooperative learning, including peer tutoring
- devaluates phonics, multiplication tables, and the facts of history
- eliminates Carnegie Units graduation requirements
- creates certificates of mastery (CIM)
- forces a new "politically correct" curriculum
- aligns itself with a movement driven by the federal government

And, that's just the beginning. What about OBE's outcomes? Why are they called "outrageous"?

Endnotes

1. Personal interview by author with Susy (last name withheld), 9 March 1994.

2. "Values Appraisal Scale," given to students at Lakeridge High, Lake Oswego, Oregon, 27 September 1993.

3. Vincent Carroll, "Educators Who Deprecate Knowledge Have Lesson To Learn," *Rocky Mountain News*, 21 October 1993, A7, and Vincent Carroll, "In Littleton, Colo., Voters Expel Education Faddists," *Wall Street Journal*, 18 November 1993, A20.

4. Statement by an Oklahoma City elementary public school teacher, as transcribed by Carol Belt, 9 February 1993.

5. Jean A. King and Karen M. Evans, "Can We Achieve Outcome-Based Education?" *Educational Leadership* (October 1989): 73.

6. "Outcome-Based Education, Summary of Remarks by William J. Bennett," *Empower America* (27 May 1993): 1–2.

7. Thomas Sowell, *Inside American Education: The Deception, The Dogmatics* (New York: The Free Press, 1993), 3.

8. Daniel J. Singal, "The Other Crisis in American Education," *The Atlantic Monthly* (November 1993): 65.

9. Restructuring, using OBE, isn't limited to the classroom. Picture OBE as the bulbous head of an octopus, with education restructuring as its tentacles. Like an octopus, both head (OBE) and tentacles (restructuring) are closely intertwined. Therefore, throughout this book, OBE and education restructuring will be referred to interchangeably—as one leviathan.

10. William G. Spady, "It's Time to Take a Close Look at Outcome-Based Education," *Outcomes* (Summer 1992): 8, 12, 13.

11. Sandy Garrett, "Learner Outcomes, Oklahoma State Competencies Grades Six-Twelve," (Oklahoma State Department of Education, n.d.), iii.

12. David T. Kearns, "Toward a New Generation of American Schools," *Phi Delta Kappan* (June 1993): 774.

13. *Arkansas Learner Outcomes: A Vision For Outcomes-Based Education*, Arkansas Department of Education (September 1991).

14. "Alabama Gap Analysis: Developing a Blueprint for Education Reform" (n.p., n.d.): 100–101.

15. *Learning A Living: A Blueprint for High Performance: A SCANS Report for Goals 2000* (U.S. Department of Labor, April 1992), xix.

16. Lynn Olson, "Center Presses 'Certificate of Initial Mastery'," *Education Week* (20 April 1994): 1, 11.

17. Kentucky House Bill 940, Section 7.

18. Paul Greenberg, "Adventures in Education," *Greensboro News and Record*, 3 February 1994, A13.

19. Thomas Sowell, "Tragicomedy," *Forbes* (6 June 1994): 52.

20. Spady, "Close Look," 6.

21. Ibid., 6-13, and Ron Brandt, "On Outcome-Based Education: A Conversation with Bill Spady," *Educational Leadership* (December 1992/January 1993): 67.

22. Spady, "Close Look," 6.

23. Holly Holland, "Sponsors Call Off Spelling Bees," *Louisville Courier-Journal*, 5 December 1993, B1, 6.

24. Lucy May, "New Letters on Report Cards Spell C-O-N-F-U-S-I-O-N for Parents," *Lexington Herald-Leader*, 1 February 1994, 1.

25. Holland, "Sponsors Call Off Spelling Bees," B1.

26. Alan November, "The Promised Land," *Electronic Learning* (September 1992): 20.

27. Phone interview by author with David Johnson, dean of students for twelve years, now a counselor at a Bay City public school, 22 September 1994.

28. "What Did You Learn in School Today?" Channel 4 News, Oklahoma City, OK, 12 March 1993.

29. William G. Spady and Kit J. Marshall, "Beyond Traditional Outcome-Based Education," *Educational Leadership* (October 1991): 70, 71.

30. William G. Spady, "Future Trends: Considerations in Developing Exit Outcomes," *High Success Program on Outcome-Based Education* (September 1987): 3.

31. Partial listing of questions from "Bettendorf Survey," given to high school students in Bettendorf, Iowa, 1992.

32. David Krathwohl, Benjamin S. Bloom, and Bertram B. Mascia, *Taxonomy of Educational Objectives Handbook II: Affective Domain* (New York: David McKay Company, Inc.).

33. Susan Walton, "There Has Been a Conspiracy of Silence About Teaching," *Education Week* (31 August 1983): 5.

34. Brandt, "A Conversation with Bill Spady," 66.

35. Heidi Mae Bratt and Anne Fracassa, "Grading Kids Goes Beyond ABCs," *Detroit News*, 3 February 1993.

36. Krathwohl, Bloom, and Mascia, *Taxonomy*, 55.

37. Benjamin S. Bloom, *All Our Children Learning: A Primer for Parents, Teachers, and Other Educators* (New York: McGraw–Hill Book Company, 1981), 180.

38. Dr. William Spady, Overhead transparency, 1990.

39. The Ohio Education Goals & Strategies Commission. n.d.

40. Brandt, "A Conversation with Bill Spady," 68, and grant proposal, "Research and Dissemination of Exemplary Outcome-Based Programs" (Far West Laboratory for Education and Research and Development, 1984), 2.

41. George N. Schmidt, "Chicago Mastery Reading," *Learning* (November 1982): 37.

42. Ibid., 38.

43. Grant proposal cover letter to U. S. Secretary of Education T. H. Bell from Utah State Superintendent of Public Instruction G. Leland Burningham, 27 July 1984. And "National, Western Region, Utah," is listed on the grant's Federal Assistance Standard Form 424, under "Area of Project Impact" (1 August 1984).

44. Center School, New Canaan, Connecticut; Johnson City Central School District, New York; Red Bank Borough School District, New Jersey.

45. According to the 1983–1984 New Canaan Public Schools School Directory.

46. Robert Burns, "Models of Instructional Organization: A Casebook on Mastery Learning and Outcome-Based Education," Far West Laboratory for Educational Research and Development (April 1987): 126.

47. Johnson City Central School, New York, which uses OBE's Outcome Driven Developmental Model (ODDM). See chapter 10 for details about ODDM.

48. *Five Lectures by James M. Gustafson, Richard S. Peters, Lawrence Kohlberg, Bruno Bettelheim, Kenneth Keniston on Moral Education with an Introduction by Nancy F. and Theodore R. Sizer* (Massachusetts: A Harvard Paperback, 1970), 3.

49. John Goodlad, "Report of President's Commission on School Finance" (Department of Health, Education and Welfare, 1970), 13, 14.

50. Ira Magaziner and Hillary Rodham Clinton, "Will America Choose High Skills or Low Wages?" *Education Leadership* (March 1992): 2.

51. *SCANS*, xvi.

52. Phyllis Schlafly, "What's Wrong With Outcome-Based Education?" *The Phyllis Schlafly Report* (May 1993).

53. "Ohio: A Community of Learners" (Ohio Schools Development Corporation, Battelle Institute, Ohio Department of Education), ii.

54. Dr. Richard J. Reif and Gail M. Morse, "Restructuring the Science Classroom," *T.H.E. Journal* (April 1992): 69.

TWO

OUTRAGEOUS OUTCOMES

It was merely a question of learning to think as they [the Party] thought.

—George Orwell, *1984*

Taking Outcomes Shopping

Karen stares out the pharmacy window. Tears of embarrassment blur her vision of Jefferson, Kentucky's beautiful bluegrass countryside. At the counter, three high-school classmates giggle while filling in their homework sheet. It says, "List three kinds of latex condoms and the prices for each product." Excitedly they circle "Yes" on question four, "Would you recommend that a friend buy protection here?"

These three collaborative learners playfully nudge each other, each thinking that their parents would just die, if they knew.

This assignment conjures up images of actually using what they're pricing. Images that otherwise wouldn't be so personalized. Their mental pictures are far different from the rolling mountains filling Karen's gaze.

"Hey, Karen, think you can handle completing the assignment by filling in the store's name and when it's open for business?" they laugh.

And, they joke about "Karen the prude," remembering her discomfort last week when the class homework assignment was to *Visit a Clinic*—a family planning clinic. Everyone had to report how much the "clinic's" birth-control

29

information costs. To make sure students like Karen got the message, instructions required students to write whether they would or would not recommend the clinic to a friend and tell why or why not. They couldn't skip going and just copy the information from a friend. Small print at the bottom of the homework sheet said, "Reminder: Attach a card from the clinic."

Karen's name is fictitious. But, *Visit a Clinic* and *Shopping Information Form* are real homework assignments in Jefferson County. They help students meet Kentucky's Valued Outcome: #49: "Students will demonstrate the ability to assess and access health systems, services and resources available in their community which maintain and promote healthy living for its citizens."[1]

Webster defines *outcome* as "result; consequence."[2] How does OBE define *outcome*?

Defining *Outcomes*

"Defining 'outcomes' has become the new education game in the 1990s." So says the *Wall Street Journal* in an article called, "The Inevitable Outcome of 'Outcomes.' " *Outcomes* used to mean what children actually learned.[3] Under this new education reform, *outcome* means "mathematicians would have our students learn 'to think mathematically,' without bothering to learn the multiplication table."[4] Outcomes now promote controversial philosophies, such as "all students shall succeed" without the rigors of competition, combined with a liberal social agenda. Egalitarianism and political correctness rule the day.

But, aren't test scores outcomes? Isn't recognizing Beethoven's "Moonlight Sonata" an outcome? No, not according to OBE's definition. OBE guru, Dr. Spady, says an outcome is not a concept, or a grade or test score, "but an *actual demonstration* in an *authentic context*" (emphasis in original).[5] What does that mean—not in "educababble"—but in plain English?

Outcomes are real life demonstrations, not classroom knowledge. "Authentic context" might mean measuring a bridge or changing oil in a car; outcomes prepare future workers for a global society.

In Ohio, one outcome is "Make decisions that conserve and enhance the natural environment."[6] To meet this outcome, Centerville fourth-graders rolled up sleeves on their new Save-the-Rain Forest T-shirts, grabbed dust rags, and spent a morning polishing furniture at a local store—which refuses to sell products made of rain forest woods.[7] After this "actual demonstration" in an "authentic context," while sitting on sofas, these nine-year-olds were given a lecture on conserving the rain forest. "They [children] have a lot of influence over their parents," said the delighted store owner.[8]

Typical of many outcomes, an OBE school in Danvers, Massachusetts, lists among its "exit outcomes":[9]

- Self-Esteem (which includes, "reflects positive self-image")
- Essential Knowledge (which includes, "accepts responsibility for the environment" and "appreciates the concept of global inter-dependence")
- Critical/Creative Thinking (which includes, "tolerates reasonable ambiguity")
- Personal/Social Management (which includes, "exhibits willingness to compromise" and "realizes that what is considered 'normal' is relative")

How would a teacher without a degree in psychology evaluate "reflects positive self-image"? Which perspective should be used to assess "accepts responsibility for the environment"—Green Peace or Mobil Corporation? Are "tolerates reasonable ambiguity" (whatever that means) and "realizes that what is considered 'normal' is relative" *academic* outcomes? These "exit outcomes" will soon change graduation requirements. Demonstrating mastery of outcomes will be the new standard for exiting from high school.

An OBE magazine, *Outcomes*, adds that an outcome is a "demonstration of three things: knowledge, competence .ı. . and 'orientations' " (orientations are defined as attitudes).[10] Education based on outcomes thrusts curriculum into a domain of changing knowledge, behaviors, and attitudes.

In other words, children must *know*, *do* and *be like* whatever the outcome stipulates.

Changing Attitudes

To *do* means to perform or demonstrate an outcome. For example, those Kentucky students actually priced condoms and were required to walk into a family-planning clinic. *Be like* is synonymous with attitudes or personal values. In this case, *be like* is assessed by students circling, from one to four, their level of comfort in the clinic. Students are then required to expose their attitudes (be like) by writing two sentences revealing why they "would/wouldn't tell a friend to visit this clinic for a consultation about protection."[11]

Outcomes are specific goals, often intended to change attitudes. Lest you think you might opt your child out of this kind of assignment, OBE always integrates courses (e.g., social studies/English/science taught together). Kentucky's Valued Outcome #49, about accessing and assessing local health systems, may be mixed into several courses such as personal wellness, ecology, or consumerism. How would a parent opt his child out of all those courses?

Parents don't object to schools teaching values or changing behavior. Schools have always encouraged children not to cheat or run in the hallways. That's behavioral instruction. However, many outcomes delve into *affective* education. *Affective* pertains to emotions or attitudes, rather than thought. It's appropriate for students to learn about the rain forest and China's overpopulation, but should children be taught, tested, then retested on "proper" attitudes (personal values) toward such issues?

For example, in Iowa, a draft version of that state's outcomes includes "Environmental Responsibility." The obvious politically correct bias of this outcome is especially striking because of the absence of any outcomes relating to "economic responsibility."

"Changing Values" is the title of a student worksheet from Iowa. Its introduction tells pupils, "The values of past generations do not always meet our present needs." The worksheet explains that although some old values are still held, others have been replaced with "new values." Students are told either to write "no change" or to explain what caused the "new value" change. Look at just three of these "old" American beliefs:

2. People ought to have large families.

4. Everyone has the right to have as many children as he or she wants.

6. Americans have a right to the resources of the world.[12]

Outcomes require demonstration of attitudes about environment and population control. However, doesn't the First Amendment permit a student to have "no attitude at all" if he or she so desires?

Twinkies and Purple Shoes

Ohio. July 1992. A Learner Outcome Panel releases a list of "indicators" for measuring how students can demonstrate (or *be like*) Ohio's twenty-five learner outcomes. These outcomes were to replace Ohio's current graduation requirements. One indicator is "Eat a balanced diet."[13]

No more Twinkies in junior's lunch bag: it's every mother's dream; except with outcome-based education, a student must demonstrate he is indeed eating a balanced diet. Some behavior *(be like)* must be performed, assessed, and—if needed—remediated until the desired behavior is produced. What's the difference between teaching a student about nutrition and requiring that child to eat a particular diet?

There's a major distinction between teaching that Twinkies contain fat (allowing the student to make a personal decision about eating them) and saying, if you eat Twinkies you will not graduate. Teaching information and requiring changed behavior may look the same, but, in reality, they are not.

Again, to illustrate what mandating OBE's outcomes means for an individual child, think about getting a telemarketing sales pitch in your home.

"Hi," says a smooth voice, "I'm selling purple shoes today." Then, he quickly fires three questions at you.

"Are you a shoe owner?"

"Yes," you answer.

"Do you like the color purple?" he asks.

"Yes," you mumble.

"Do you buy your own shoes, or does some other member of the family purchase shoes for you?" he asks.

"I buy my own," you answer.

The purple-shoe salesperson has just established enough baseline data to be aware of your consumer preferences (that's a pretest). Now, he can begin teaching. He'll give you ten airtight reasons why you need purple shoes—why you can't live without them. In other words, he's taught you something (that's the curriculum). You've answered his pre-test questions and listened to his curriculum. Now, he ends the sale by asking the familiar, "Would you like to put that on your VISA or Master Card?" He is assessing to see if you've met his outcome or goal. (That's the post-test.)

If you say, "Put it on my VISA," you've mastered his goal (outcome). After thanking you, he'll hang up. (That's graduation.)

But, what if you respond, "I don't want shoes"? Then, you have not met the outcome. He'll ask why not. Then, he'll put you through another salespitch to make you want purple shoes. (That's remediation.) You walk through that sales loop one more time. At the end of that "remediation," again he asks, "Shall I put this on your VISA or Master Card?" You're being tested, again. (That's assessment.) If you say, "Yes." You've graduated from the conversation, and he'll hang up. If you say, "No," he'll remediate you again. And again. And again.

If you stay on that phone indefinitely, he'll make you walk that remediation loop until you finally say, "Yes, I'll buy shoes." You must meet his outcome. However, with a telephone sales call, you can say, "Excuse me, I've been remediated enough. I'll never buy your shoes." Click, you hang up.

A child in a classroom cannot hang up the phone. She is going to be remediated again, and again, and again, until she meets the outcomes.

Redefining Special Ed

To graduate, your child must meet all the outcomes. Opting out of one, even if your family finds it objectionable, isn't allowed. All children must meet all outcomes to graduate.

What if a student can achieve fifty-two goals, but fifty-three are required? Officials say that youngster could have a special education plan written for him. But, if every child who doesn't meet the outcomes is declared "special ed," officials now have rerouted funding away from children who have legitimate problems—and have redefined special education.

The barriers between general and special education "must be eliminated," demands an influential pro-OBE publication.[14] Following that edict, across the nation special ed children are being "mainstreamed" into regular classrooms. Certified school psychologist Steven Kossor states, "There is very little difference between OBE regulations and the special education regulations governing Individual Education Plans (IEPs)."[15]

How does "mainstreaming" fit into the OBE agenda? 1) Money formerly spent on special ed now goes into general classes (OBE is expensive); 2) previously only special ed children used Individual Education Plans (IEPs), but now IEPs will be developed for all students; and 3) a special education student will be redefined as a child who can't, or chooses not to, meet the outcomes.

Academic Bankruptcy

Meeting outcomes dramatically affects each child in the classroom. But, outcomes are also a sword hanging over the heads of teachers, administrators, and school board members. What happens if your school district chooses not

to meet the state's outcomes (often called performance standards)?

According to OBE's "reward and punishment" plan,
the state will march in and take over the school. If a school
fails to meet outcomes, the state has the power to dismiss
personnel (teacher tenure is "modified") and to suspend
elected school boards, replacing them with appointed officials. In Pennsylvania, this pending legislation is called "Academic Bankruptcy."[16]

Unfortunately, in many states, "academic bankruptcy"
(called by various names) is now law. For example, in Massachusetts it's called "under-performing."[17] The *Boston Globe*
reports that this punishment section was passed as part of
the Education Reform Act of 1993. Now, in schools which
that state deems "under-performing," even principals can
be removed.[18] In March 1994, Massachusetts' thirty-nine
outcomes (called Common Core) included being able to
"identify stereotyping," "understand human sexuality," and
"use appropriate gestures."[19] How would teachers grade a
student in "using appropriate gestures"? What if a school is
academically superior but refuses to implement an outcome
like "identifying stereotyping" as a graduation requirement?
Would that school risk a state takeover?

After four years of Kentucky's outcome-based reform,
about two-thirds of its schools *are* in some danger of state
takeover.[20] In 1994, Kentucky's Commissioner of Education
Thomas Boysen warned that, "under the reform act,
schools . . . can be declared 'schools in crisis' and face state
takeover."[21] His hit list included the Bluegrass State's top
school, Ballard High. Although Ballard had produced twenty-
one National Merit Scholarship semifinalists that year, the
Courier-Journal reported that "if dramatic progress isn't made
by next year, the state could declare Ballard . . . in crisis."[22]

Nationwide, education restructuring bills include this
"punishment." It's called by various names, such as: "School
in Crisis" (Kentucky), "Public Act 25, Accreditation Section
1280" (Michigan), "Academically Deficient" (Missouri), "Deficient" (Oregon).

Outcome-based education doesn't just break the mold of America's traditional schools; it empowers the state to usurp control.

One State's Outcomes

What are OBE's outcomes? Why might a child or a school object to mastering them? That's what citizens in Iowa wanted to know. Using traditional education, Iowa students outscored the rest of the states on the Scholastic Aptitude Tests (SATs).[23] Why would Iowa fix an education system that clearly wasn't broken? Why consider changing graduation requirements to education based on outcomes, unless those outcomes required more academic rigor? Is it possible that all states are being "softened up" for federal tests, federal certificates (a national "diploma" called the Certificate of Initial Mastery—CIM), and federal outcomes?

Many states, such as Iowa, base outcomes on national goals. "The state outcomes will be related to, but not limited to, the six national education goals," admitted an Iowa Department of Education manual in 1992.[24] (See chapter 5 for details.) Like so many other states, Iowa's outcomes are the hub of a "new" education system.[25]

Also called "Ideal Schools," this "new" system calls for an ungraded primary school through fifth grade, prekindergarten for all four-year-olds, special ed changes, teachers becoming facilitators, computers for every student, tech prep, youth apprenticeships, site-based management— and family resource centers in every community, close to or in a school.[26] According to legislation mandating family resource centers, these centers may "provide an adolescent pregnancy prevention program."[27]

Since Iowa's documents also link their "Ideal Schools" to Ira Magaziner's report, *America's Choice*, it's likely Iowa also may create a Certificate of Initial Mastery of the outcomes.[28] Will Iowa's "new" system of outcomes fine-tune academics?

"Remember the television fast-food hamburger advertisement which aired a few years ago?" asks Sarah, an Iowa parent. "A grandmother-type woman lifts her hamburger bun and yells, 'Where's the beef?' Well, I'm demanding, 'Where's the academics?' "

Some of Iowa's outcomes (also called "results") sound academic, but many raise red flags for citizens like Sarah:

Communication

Problem Solving

Lifelong Learning

Commitment to Quality

Creativity

Life Management

Diversity

Environmental Responsibility

Group Membership[29]

"I guess communications means reading and writing. Problem solving demands computing and science," Sarah says. But, she wonders after those two, how will teachers score lifelong learning or group membership? "Look at the list. These outcomes open up a Pandora's Box of dangerous possibilities."

She adds, "If you ask the average person what he or she wants educational outcomes to be, you'll almost never hear diversity, environmental responsibility or group membership." She glances at her three-year-old flipping pages in *The Cat in the Hat.* "What most Americans want is reading, writing, math, science, and other academic subjects. Values are for us as parents to instill."[30]

Copycat Outcomes

In 1991, a group of Pennsylvania concerned citizens demanded, "Where did our state's outcomes come from?"

Officials from the Department of Education explained they had appointed eleven task forces to prepare drafts of Student Learning Outcomes. Obviously, each task force worked hard to hammer out outcomes specifically for the Keystone State.

"Were our outcomes drafted from scratch?" pressed parents. "Was the table empty?"

"Well, we did have Connecticut's outcomes," mumbled the officials.

So, citizens contacted Connecticut and studied its outcomes, called "Common Core of Learning." What they discovered was that Pennsylvania had adopted Connecticut's goals, practically verbatim.

Pennsylvania Outcomes	Connecticut Outcomes
All students develop personal criteria for making informed moral judgments and ethical decisions.	Each student should be able to develop personal criteria for making informed moral judgments and ethical decisions.
Each student should be able to develop an understanding of his/her strengths and weaknesses and the ability to maximize strengths and rectify or compensate for weaknesses.	All students develop an understanding of their strengths and weaknesses and the ability to maximize strengths and compensate for weaknesses.
Each student should be able to strive toward and take the risks necessary for accomplishing tasks and fulfilling ambitions.	All students take the risks necessary for accomplishing tasks and fulfilling personal ambitions.

"Was the table empty?" asked taxpayers and parents from the OBE states of Kansas and Oklahoma. When they compared their outcomes, here is what they found:[31]

Kansas Exit Outcomes	Oklahoma Exit Outcomes
1. Schools have a basic mission which prepares the learners to live, learn, and work in a global society.	1. Schools have a basic mission which prepares the learners to live, learn, and work in a global society.

2. Students have the communication skills necessary to live, learn, and work in a global society.

2. Students have the communication skills necessary to live, learn, and work in the 21st century.

3. Students think creatively and problem solve in order to live, learn, and work in a global society.

3. Students think creatively and problem solve in order to live, learn, and work in the 21st century.

4. Students have the physical and emotional well-being necessary to live, learn, and work in a global society.

4. Students have the physical and emotional well-being necessary to live, learn, and work in the 21st century.

5. Students participate in lifelong learning.

5. Students participate in lifelong learning as contributing members of a community of learners.

Americans pride themselves on their rugged independence, their individuality, even their contrariness. Each state is separate, yet united by a common national allegiance. This sameness of outcomes in all states smacks of conformity.

If outcomes were predominately academic, such as "must read to the tenth grade level," each state would adopt a similar goal. But, why are states cranking out the same nonacademic goals like "lifelong learner," "community contributor," "quality producer"?

Such outcomes *mandate* uniform attitudes and behavior. That goes against American individualism. It flies in the face of states' rights, of an individual's rights.

If outcomes fail in one state, the nation bleeds. If all states require the same non-cognitive outcomes—and OBE fails—our nation will hemorrhage.

Local Outcome Planning

Before a state drafts outcomes, OBE is planted throughout its school districts. A mix of about thirty teachers, school directors, parents, and community members are appointed to a strategic planning committee. They're a group with much power, but no responsibility to an electorate.

Local school boards have always controlled the goals of each district. But, now the school directors take a back seat while an unelected strategic planning group writes the district's all-important outcomes. And, the *Wall Street Journal* adds that new parent-councils at every school will "take over much of the power wielded by local school boards."[32]

An attitude among OBE promoters toward school boards is "Go away Philistines who manage schools."[33] Alan November, in his article "The Promised Land," says it is a number one priority that "champions of the old cultural values" (school boards) must be eliminated.[34] Why?

"Traditional values are an obstacle to OBE education," explains John, a strategic planning committee member. When he tried to introduce Judeo/Christian beliefs, he discovered this was not a group of people around a table simply sharing ideas about outcomes. "I found it was a tightly controlled setting designed to force consensus."

Although the group appears to reach "consensus," outcomes are usually predetermined by the group's facilitator. Often their table is not empty. Even if a community comes up with its own outcomes, each district's strategic plan must be sent to the state's department of education for approval.

So much for OBE's rhetoric about local control for designing outcomes. Communities are invited to come up with any plan they choose, as long as that plan looks exactly like what the state wants. John's comment is, "It's like the state saying 'here's a Cessna airplane. Use any design you want as long as in the end your plan is a Cessna airplane.'"

Kentucky: OBE Lighthouse

This chapter began with an example from Kentucky because the *Washington Times* says, "Outcome-based advocates use Kentucky as Exhibit A."[35] According to the state-education mission statement, Kentucky is "the national catalyst for education transformation."[36] U.S. Secretary of Education Richard Riley agrees, calling Kentucky a "lighthouse of reform" for the rest of the nation.[37] (It's fascinating that across the nation, every school, every district, every state is told the same thing: "you're a 'pilot,' you're on the 'cutting edge,' your outcomes are unique.")

However, a few states like Oregon and Kentucky actually did get a jump-start on OBE. When the Bluegrass State's legislature passed the massive 1990 Kentucky Education Reform Act (KERA), no outcomes were in sight. Although KERA mandated performance-based education, it was the unelected bureaucrats at the Department of Education (DOE) who drafted seventy-five Learner Outcomes afterward.

Kentucky now publishes a state curriculum framework. (A state curriculum is unusual. Historically in America, each district has decided how to frame its own curriculum to meet specific local needs.) *Transformations: Kentucky's Curriculum Framework* claims "it is not mandatory . . . [but] it does offer assistance . . . to meet the state's 75 outcomes." This inch-thick, detailed manual suggests teaching activities to meet outcomes. Below are some examples:

> • "Research the impact that various interest groups (e.g., Act-up, National Organization for Women, UNICEF) have had on science-related discoveries, inventions, or cures. Join or contribute to one of these organizations."[38]

This is specified for middle-school science class. Ask yourself what impact Act-up (activist homosexual group) has had on discoveries or inventions? Aren't its members spreading, not curing, several venereal diseases including AIDS? Why encourage young adolescents to "join or contribute to" a militant homosexual group like Act-up? This application was deleted after loud parental protest. But, other objectionable applications remain, such as:

> • "Examine the mental and emotional wellness of . . . past or present world leaders."[39]

Since this is a social studies "application," why not study Christopher Columbus' or Thomas Jefferson's contributions?

Why force students to psychoanalyze leaders' emotional health. This wastes valuable class time, and it degrades history.

> • "Research as a class the issue of teenage suicide by engaging . . . in the following activities: Read a novel and watch a movie that focuses on teenage suicide. Interview parents of teenage suicide victims."[40]

Fixating on suicide destroys rather than improves a child's emotional health. One teenager in a Pennsylvania OBE school watched a movie about suicide. He went straight home and imitated what he learned during the film. But, rather than taking only a few pills, as the movie depicted, he swallowed them all.[41]

National Outcomes

Today, outcomes are dark clouds moving in fast-forward motion. Not only is Kentucky called a "lighthouse," Secretary Riley also says President Clinton's Goals 2000: Educate America Act would help states "duplicate what Kentucky has done and is doing."[42] Using these federal bills as incentives, the government will fill its bureaucratic lungs and blow—pushing at hurricane speed—outcomes into every state.

Therefore, watch for national outcomes. They're being developed now. They will probably be called national "performance standards."

In 1992, an $8.5 million grant was given to develop national tests. "National standards [outcomes] and tests are necessary for a couple of reasons," explains Jim Gilchrist, operations director of the project. The main reason? He says that children are the future workforce and must be "trained."[43] (You train a dog. You educate a child.)

"Outcomes are already found in nationally-distributed OBE curricula," observes Dr. Jeffrey Burke Satinover, a psychiatrist who also holds a master's in education from Harvard. "The result will be children who all have been trained to think the same way about major social questions."[44]

The "New Basics"

Children will learn politically correct attitudes through the "new basics."

When OBE advocates talk about the "new basics," they mean outcomes. Why do outcomes stress teaching multiculturalism, working well in groups, and self-esteem, as much as, say, mathematics? Perhaps well-known reading specialist Thomas G. Sticht can shed light on this question. In 1987, he said,

> Many companies have moved operations to places with cheap, relatively poorly educated labor. What may be crucial, they say, is the dependability of a labor force and how well it can be managed and trained—not its general education level, although a small cadre of highly educated creative people is essential to innovation and growth. Ending discrimination and *changing values* are probably *more important than reading* in moving low-income families into the middle class (emphasis added).[45]

Sticht, Spady, Sizer, Magaziner, H. Clinton, and others promoting this movement are, no doubt, part of the "small cadre of highly educated creative people" essential for growth. Sticht was a member of the U.S. Labor Department's *Secretary's Commission on Achieving Necessary Skills (SCANS)*.

According to the *Washington Times*, the "*SCANS* directives tell schools how they ought to instill 'workplace competencies' in pupils at every level of instruction."[46] Under Workplace Competencies, the *SCANS* lists: sociability, reading, problem solving, decision making, self-esteem, and self-management.[47] Would a shy, independent student like Albert Einstein have met all the outcomes—including the "new basic" of sociability?

Old Face, New Name

Outcome-based education is ever changing, evolving. An article entitled "Beyond Traditional Outcome-Based Education" says outcome-based education's name can evolve;

it can operate under many labels—"Mastery Learning, Out-come-Based Instruction, Outcomes Driven Developmental Model, OBE, or something else."[48] Kentucky's "something else" is "Performance-Based Education"—the same name used in the GOALS 2000: Educate America Act.

KERA's outcomes evolved through three or four name changes: "Valued Outcomes" to "Learner Outcomes" to "Academic Expectations." Notice "Academic Expectations" deletes the increasingly controversial word *outcomes*. Al-though the latest name may sound new it will still recycle the same outcomes. In the words of a Kentucky Depart-ment of Education publication, these new, forty-student "Aca-demic Expectations" are "consistent with the intentions of the original outcomes."[49] Old face, new name.

Ohio. After two years of loud public outcry against out-comes in the Buckeye State, the head of the Department of Education wrote a letter saying mistakes were made and he wanted to "drive a stake through the heart of OBE."[50] But, according to Ohio State Rep. Michael Wise, the DOE con-tinued the work of drafting goals and outcomes.[51] Now, "learner outcomes" are relabeled under a new name, "Rep-resentative Indicators." Old face, new name.

Indiana's Hoosiers are shooting hoops while citizens are finding that "locally developed" outcomes coinciden-tally match the draft form of the state's *Curriculum Develop-ment Framework: Guide to a School Based Process*. To diffuse public protest, some localities change the label Outcome-Based Education (OBE) to Outcome Aligned Education (OAE). Old face, new name.

Meanwhile, the Evergreen State of Washington sends draft number eight of its Performance-Based Education Act (H.B. 1209) back to the drawing board. The law had de-fined outcome-based and performance-based education iden-tically—" 'Performance-based' or 'outcome-based' education means a system designed to meet specific objectives or standards of what students should know and be able to do."[52] To assuage public protest against OBE, the final ver-sion of their education bill quietly deletes from its definition of "performance-based education," "outcome-based." However, the intent is clear. (By the way, in this bill, Washington State joins Oregon and Massachusetts in mandating a Certificate of Mastery.) Old face, new name.

Why are local districts and states playing the shell game with the word *outcome*? This plan to destroy America's traditional schools is too well financed, too carefully planned, too close to completion to allow mere citizens to stop it.

Name Calling

The *Washington Times* on 1 April 1994 had a name for Virginia's OBE outcomes—"feel-good education." Albert Shanker calls OBE's outcomes, "Outrageous."[53] Strong reaction—especially from the president of America's second largest teachers' union, the American Federation of Teachers. Shanker doesn't mince words about OBE. He says Americans are correctly suspicious of OBE's outcomes. Not only are they academically "fluffy," but they intrude into the sanctity of the American home.

In his *New York Times* article, Shanker quotes a few "learner outcomes." One of Ohio's outcomes requires a graduate to "function as a responsible family member." Shanker, who is no right-winger, applauds ultra right-wing groups for actively opposing OBE. "The radical right has a point when it worries that a school will try to find out whether a student is a 'responsible family member.' This kind of outcome may encourage schools to indoctrinate youngsters about family styles that run counter to their religious beliefs."[54]

Outcomes such as "understand human diversity" encourage tolerance for all lifestyles and religious groups, except for the two capital C groups—Conservatives and Christians. Did you notice that Albert Shanker calls opponents of OBE "ultra right-wingers"? Evidently he buys into pro-OBE rhetoric. OBE's propaganda constantly spits out articles, seminars, and books informing the wide-eyed public that only "fringe," right-wing groups oppose outcomes.

The National Education Association even funded a nearly two-hundred-page manual for educators experiencing "problems" with parents opposing reform. Under the section, "Profile of a Censor" (page 25), the "far right" are "good, salt of the earth, concerned parents" who are "absolutists in their beliefs." Listed in Selected Leaders of the Far Right (page 29) are Ronald Reagan, Phyllis Schlafly, William Bennett, and Jesse Helms. The book title shows how destructive William Bennett and "salt of the earth parents" are perceived to be: *What's Left After the Right?*[55]

It's smart in a culture war to label your enemy so he can be mocked, then discredited. Smart, yes. Tolerant, no. Ironically, the understand-human-diversity theme is built into everyone's outcomes. Yet, across the country, if you question OBE, you'll intolerantly be branded "Christian Far Right" and dismissed.

It doesn't matter if you're an atheist or a Hindu or a Jew. Why would a political bent or religious belief affect your right to protest in America? "Shouldn't a conservative enjoy the same right to voice an opinion as any other individual?" demands anti-OBE activist Joel. He believes the term *Christian Far Right* has been marketed so cleverly that everyone thinks it's synonymous with "kook." "No matter how well I document where OBE is failing academically, I'm not taken seriously since I'm now labeled 'Christian Far Right!' " says Joel, who's Jewish.

Name That Tune: "All Must Succeed"

Repeating a phrase over and over, such as Christian Far Right, is a common marketing technique that uses mnemonics. It helps one remember an idea without thinking. When you hear, "Just Do It," "Reach Out and Touch Someone," "Safe Sex," or "Catch the Wave," you picture Nike, AT&T, condoms, and Coke—not what those phrases mean literally. Mnemonics often make you feel, not think.

Phrases repeated over and over by those marketing outcome-based education are: "All students shall succeed," "Success breeds success," and "It takes a village to raise a child." Because the mnemonic technique is so effective, teachers, administrators, and the media repeat these slogans with parrot-like enthusiasm.

If a saying has a nice ring to it, it doesn't necessarily mean it rings true. For instance, "All students shall succeed," literally means *no* student shall fail. It implies failure is harmful, not an incentive to try harder. "Success breeds success," tells teachers to create "success" by inflating grades. If everyone is getting *A*s and *B*s, then OBE must be working. Tell a mother in inner-city Chicago, "It takes a village to raise a child." Her village is filled with drug dealers and pedophiles. "Outcomes will create world class education," chant OBE promoters. It has been said, you shouldn't confuse a slogan with a solution.

Yesterday's Outcomes vs. OBE Outcomes

Are the outcomes used in performance-based or outcome-based education, world class? The *Wall Street Journal* printed an 1885 examination for admission to Jersey City High School.[56] Compare Jersey City's 1885 "outcomes" with

1880s—Yesterday's "Outcomes" (8th grade) New Jersey	1990s—Today's "Outcomes" (K-12) Minnesota
• Define Algebra, an algebraic expression, a polynomial. Make a literal trinomial.	• Participate in lifelong learning.
• Write a homogeneous quadrinomial of the third degree. Express the cube root of 10ax in two ways.	• Examine personal beliefs and values and their relationship to behavior.
• Express the following in its simplest form by removing the parentheses and combining: 1-(1-a)+(1-a+a)-(1-a+a-a).	• Make ethical and moral decisions.
• What is the axis of the earth? What is the equator? What is the distance from the equator to either pole in	• Be a responsible citizen of the community, nation, and the world.
	• Practice stewardship of the land, natural resources, and environment.
	• Accept that there is more than one way of being human.

degrees, in miles? Why is it warmer at the equator than near the poles?

• Name four principal ranges of mountains in Asia, three in Europe, and three in Africa.

• Name the capitals of the following countries: Portugal, Greece, Egypt, Japan, China, Canada, Tibet, Cuba.

• Name the states on the west bank of the Mississippi, and the capital of each.

• Resolve conflict in the manner most beneficial to society.

• Develop a feeling of positive self-worth, security, and self-assurance.

• Tolerate ambiguity.

• Make informed decisions about health products and services.

1991 "Model Learner Outcomes for International Education" printed by Minnesota's Department of Education.[57]

Summing Up Outcomes

To sum up, listen to a Kentucky teacher, Eddie Price, discuss his experience with "today's outcomes." Throughout Eddie's seventeen years of teaching, he has been showered with state Excellence in Teaching commendations and high school Teacher of the Year awards.[58]

Eddie is an enthusiastic optimist. At first, he supported the Kentucky Education Reform Act and even developed a state award-winning curriculum. Yet, while promotional pictures of students in his classroom were being faxed across the state, Eddie's trust in KERA was eroding.

The state had passed down a list of seventy-five state-mandated Valued Outcomes. He objected to the Department of Education's order that all curricula, all teaching—everything—had to revolve around meeting these Valued Outcomes:

> Valued Outcomes were soon labeled "Learner Outcomes," to quiet concerned citizens. It was this instant relabeling that first alarmed me. KERA's out-

comes appeared to throw hard, factual subject matter out the window in favor of affective goals [emotions and feelings].

We [teachers] were directed by the state to "weed out unimportant material" that did not meet the Outcomes. Our Commissioner of Education announced schools would be accountable for meeting the Outcomes. Or else. We were told, "a Kentucky Distinguished Educator will be sent to your building to help you grow." Then I learned this official had the absolute power to declare our school a "School in Crisis!" The principal and individual teachers could be eliminated with the single stroke of a pen.

Our local elected school boards were virtually stripped of their power, while state control drastically tightened. The state now mandates the outcomes and approves the curriculum.

Once I was accused of being "over-zealous" in trying to implement KERA. [Now] I'm battling alone—one small voice in a wilderness of state-controlled propaganda. This monster is so huge. I can only share my own un-mandated thoughts in the hope that others will listen and act.[59]

"One more thing," adds this respected teacher, "Our state assessment testing is insane. It's mad, mad, mad testing."

Endnotes

1. "Kentucky's Learning Goals and Valued Outcomes: Technical Report" (Council for School Performance Standards, 1 September 1991), 11.

2. *Webster's New World Dictionary*, s.v. "Outcome."

3. Irving Kristol, "The Inevitable Outcome of 'Outcomes,'" *Wall Street Journal*, 18 April 1994, A14.

4. Ibid.

5. William G. Spady, "It's Time to Take a Close Look at Outcome-Based Education," *Outcomes* (Summer 1992): 6, 7.

6. The Ohio Education Goals & Strategies Commission, *Learner Outcomes*.

7. Katherine Ullmer, "Students Polish Off Cleaning Chore," *Dayton Daily*, 2 March 1984, 1, 6.

8. Ibid., 6.

9. Superintendent's Update, Danvers, Massachusetts, 30 May 1991.

10. Spady, "Look at Outcome-Based Education," *Outcomes* (Summer 1992): 6.

11. "Reducing the Risk: Building Skills to Prevent Pregnancy: STD & HIV" (Santa Cruz, CA: ETR Associates, 1993), 113, 123.

12. "Changing Values," student worksheet, 1993.

13. "Learner Outcome Panel Suspended," *Education News* (December 1993): 10, and "Preparing Ohio's Learners for the Twenty-First Century: Pre K-12 Standards, Working Draft" (Ohio Department of Education, 1 September 1993), 20.

14. Alan Gartner and Dorothy Kerzner Lipsky, *The Yoke of Special Education: How To Break It* (Rochester, NY: National Center on Education and the Economy, 1989), 31.

15. Steven Kossor, licensed psychologist, in an untitled position paper comparing OBE and special education (1992).

16. "Academic Bankruptcy," Pennsylvania Senate Bill 205 (1994 pending). Due to citizens' protest, Senate Bill 1268, an academic bankruptcy bill, was defeated in 1992. However, in 1994, "Academic Bankruptcy" appeared again.

17. The Education Reform Act of 1993 (H 1000), 13, 28.

18. Patricia Nealon, "Power Shift Being Felt in Mass. School System," *Boston Globe*, 1 August 1993, 29.

19. Jeff Jacoby, "The 39-Point Blueprint for Ignorance," *Boston Globe*, 24 March 1994.

20. Lucy May, " 'Two-Thirds Of Schools Mediocre At Best,' Boysen says," *Lexington Herald-Leader*, 18 February 1994, A1.

21. Ibid.

22. Leslie Scanlon, "High-Rated Ballard Faces Academic Crisis," *Courier-Journal*, 1 October 1993, A1. (According to this article, all faculty could be fired by the state.)

23. "Scores in SAT on Rise," *Pittsburgh Press*, 19 August 1993, 1. In 1993, Iowa's SATs average combined verbal and math scores were 1102.

24. "Education is Iowa's Future: The State Plan for Educational Excellence in the 21st Century" (Iowa Department of Education, January 1992), 3.

25. "World-Class Schools: The Iowa Initiative" (Iowa Business Education Roundtable, 1991), 18.

26. "1993 Legislative Initiatives; Adopted by the State Board of Education" (December 1992), and "Education is Iowa's Future: The State Plan for Educational Excellence in the 21st Century" (Iowa Department of Education, January 1992).

27. "House File 2467: Family Resource Center Demonstration Program" (1992), 5.

28. "World-Class Schools: The Iowa Initiative," 18.

29. "The Outcome Assessment Initiative," draft, Iowa Department of Education (Fall 1992).

30. Phone interview by author with Sarah (last name withheld), 5 July 1994.

31. A comparison between the original draft of the Kansas Quality Performance Accreditation (3-12-91) Outcomes and the original draft written and submitted by the Oklahoma Outcomes Accreditation Task Force in 1992, as reported in "Kansas Education Watch Network," *Update* (July 1993): 2.

32. Suzanne Alexander, "Schoolroom Shuffle," *Wall Street Journal*, 5 January 1993, A1, A6.

33. Alan November, "The Promised Land," *Electronic Learning* (September 1992): 20.

34. Ibid.

35. Phyllis Schlafly, "Educantoland," *Washington Times*, 5 February 1994, D1.

36. "Transformations: Kentucky's Curriculum Framework," vol. 1, Kentucky Department of Education, 1993: i.

37. Lucy May, "U.S. Education Chief Lauds Kentucky Reform," *Lexington Herald Leader*, 16 October 1993, C3.

38. "Transformations: Kentucky's Curriculum Framework:" 126. Removed.

39. Ibid., 199.

40. Ibid.

41. Mike Coleman (student's foster parent) phone interview with author, 3 February 1994.

42. May, "Lauds Kentucky Reform," C3.

43. "University Receives Grant to Develop National Testing System," (Information Legislative Service, Pennsylvania School Board Association, 9 October 1992), 12.

44. Jeffrey Burke Satinover, M.D., "OBE Analysis," *National Parents Commission* (Spring 1994): 3

45. As quoted in *U. S. Congressional Record*, House of Representatives, 23 October 1989, 3517-3519.

46. Robert Holland, "The Hushed Takeover of American Education," *Washington Times*, 25 November 1993, A19.

47. *Learning a Living: A Blueprint for High Performance: A SCANS Report for America 2000* (U.S. Department of Labor, April 1992), 83, 84.

48. William G. Spady and Kit J. Marshall, "Beyond Traditional Outcome-Based Education," *Education Leadership* (October 1991): 67.

49. "Kentucky's Learning Goals and Academic Expectations" (Kentucky Department of Education, 1994): 1.

50. Memo from Ohio Superintendent of Public Instruction Ted Sanders to Learner Outcomes Panel, 11 January 1994.

51. Michael Wise, "Outcome-Based Education is Still on State Agenda," *Sun Courier*, 17 February 1994.

52. HB 1209, 8th Draft, Sec. 101. Washington State (5), 3.

53. Albert Shanker, "Outrageous Outcomes," *New York Times*, 12 September 1993, 7.

54. Ibid.

55. Dr. Janet L. Jones, *What's Left After the Right?* (Funded by the National Education Association), 25, 29.

56. "Sharpen Your Pencil, and Begin Now," *Wall Street Journal*, 9 June 1992, A16.

57. "Model Learner Outcomes for International Education" (Minnesota Department of Education, 1991), 11, 13, 14, 15, 16.

58. Eddie Price, "Hancock Teacher Attacks Kentucky School Reform," *Hancock Clarion*, 30 December 1993, A1.

59. Phone interview by author with Eddie Price, 5 July 1994.

THREE

MAD, MAD, MAD TESTING

Besides, the Party was in the right. It must be so: how could the immortal, collective brain be mistaken? By what external standard could you check its judgments?
—George Orwell, *1984*

Before looking at OBE assessment it would be helpful to review some basic theory on the relationship between testing and curriculum.

The first and most important fact is that testing controls curriculum. What is tested and how it is scored becomes the barometer for what happens in a classroom—especially if the test is "high stakes," or is used to rate students or teachers or schools.

The Test Drives the Curriculum

As an example, let's say that every school in a district was going to be given a multiplication examination at the third grade level in March, and that the schools would be rated by their performance on that test. What would those third grade classrooms emphasize in math? Why, multiplication, of course. The test drives the curriculum.

Or, suppose that every high school in a state would be required to give seniors a test that involved testing about the American presidents, and correct order counted in the scoring. These schools would teach not just about the presidents, but their order as well. Again, the test drives the curriculum.

In OBE, the same relationship holds. Tests are based on the outcomes, and the curriculum is based on the tests. The problem is that many outcomes are not academic, so the tests are not academic, and therefore the curriculum becomes non-academic as well.

An excellent example is Pennsylvania's Educational Quality Assessment (EQA) test, which asked for—and scored—responses to such statements as "I don't receive much attention at home."[1] Outcomes included good citizenship, adaptability to change, and self-esteem. First, the test measured those areas. Then, school districts were required to use the EQA test results to plan their curriculum to correct weaknesses identified in the EQA testing. So, curriculum moved away from academics and toward the outcomes assessed by the EQA.

The test drives the curriculum. Whoever controls the test controls the curriculum, and in OBE, the state controls the test.

Pennsylvania's OBE regulations specify that all district assessment instruments must incorporate the state assessment. So, no district can move away from the state-mandated outcomes because their assessments *must* be based on those outcomes.

School districts are judged academically by how well they perform on the state assessments, so they will have to adjust their curriculums to match the test, and therefore the outcomes, mandated by the state.

The test is driving the curriculum.

Is the Test Valid?

A valid test actually measures what it claims to measure, at the level it claims to measure. A valid science test actually asks science questions, and a valid ninth-grade reading test is written at a ninth-grade reading level. The problem with OBE assessments is that they are not necessarily valid.

For example, a 1994 Pennsylvania Reading Assessment test included a question asking students what they would do if they found a sum of money in the street—keep it or turn it in.[2] Remember that this is a *reading* test. So, does a student read better if she keeps the money—or if she turns it in? (It is worth observing here that Pennsylvania does have a goal/outcome called Ethical Judgment, which the state, after parents protested, promised would never be tested.)

California assessments also included reading selections. Here the problem was that selections in both the elementary test and the high school test were written at the seventh-grade reading level.

That meant that the selection was very difficult for elementary students, so they would get lower scores, but it was very easy for high school students, so they would get higher scores.

Therefore, schools would show improvement in their scores over time, not necessarily because students were improving, but because the task got easier.

If a bureaucracy wanted to hide an academic failure, this would be a perfect method. Since state assessments are secure, or secret, it is impossible for a parent (and almost anyone else who is interested) to figure out what is happening.

Is the Test Reliable?

Reliable tests give everyone a clear picture of what is happening. In other words, the score is the same no matter who grades the paper, and everyone is graded on the same task.

That's why standardized testing is timed. If one student is given fifteen minutes and another is given an hour to complete thirty math problems, they did not take the same test. The first student had a much more difficult task, so he could not reliably be compared to the second simply on the basis of the number of correct responses.

But, OBE uses a variety of assessment methods. One is *authentic assessment*, in which students must complete a regular classroom project, rather than a standardized test.

This is not a new idea. It was tried in Britain several years ago. The poor results were discussed in the 1993 February issue of *Phi Delta Kappan*.[3] Reliability was a problem because the teachers did not all administer the assessment test identically. Some helped students who were frustrated, some gave longer time periods, and some followed the rules. Consequently, the student scores were not a reliable indicator to use in comparing student performance.

In America, the OBE portfolio assessment system has also demonstrated problems. Assessment focuses on the thought process used in arriving at the answer instead of the accuracy of the answer itself, even in math.

Aside from the obvious question of how a wrong answer can be better than a correct one (since in a real-world situation, accuracy matters), the grading of a thought process is purely subjective.

A RAND study of a portfolio assessment system piloted in Vermont documented the lack of agreement among the raters, even in math, and concluded that, for judging student performance, the scores were essentially meaningless.[4]

One of the California tests mentioned earlier also had a reliability problem. Beside each selection was a column that told students to record their thoughts, questions, comments, etc., on the selection as they read it. The students were not told that these comment columns would be graded, so a student who read without writing would be graded lower than one who jotted something down.

Does writing in the margin make someone a better reader? And how does one grade such comments in a reliable manner? The scoring becomes, then, purely the subjective opinion of the rater instead of an effective method for measuring the achievement of a student.

Politically Correct Testing

Good tests should be content-neutral; that is, they should not promote a particular political point of view through an academic instrument. But consider just these few examples from recent OBE state assessments.

In Kentucky, students were given a chart of a hypothetical classroom, which included information on the pretend students—including their names, sex, reading scores, and number of siblings.

The children were then instructed to compare the reading scores with number of siblings and to draw conclusions based on those comparisons. When the comparisons were made, the only conclusion possible was that the more siblings a student had, the lower the reading score was.[5]

This is an inculcation of a political point of view through a testing situation. Remember that the situation was hypothetical, not actual, so the numbers on which the conclusion about larger families was based were made up by those who wrote the test.

Or consider the 1993 Kansas Middle/Junior High Reading and Mathematics Assessment. In the reading selections, a young heroine is having trouble making a decision, so she considers wishing herself dead, as a way to solve everything.[6] Why plant a deathwish in vulnerable minds through mandated assessment tests?

A California test tells the story of a wife who is mistakenly told that her husband has been killed in an accident; she is thrilled that she is now free to live only for herself. Test questions emphasize that theme. Why exalt selfishness over marriage and commitment?

None of these assessment readings are content-neutral, and they are particularly insidious because a child will be concentrating on answering the questions instead of evaluating the material contained in those questions. That material then becomes something that they (attentively) have read somewhere, which they may internalize without thinking about it.

If your goal is to change an attitude, this is a good way to do it.

Why Test?

A test is like a thermometer. It tells the tester exactly where the entity being tested is in relationship to the desired outcome.

For example, if the desired outcome is that Mrs. Jones's third graders will know their multiplication tables, and a test shows that 90 percent of the children can't solve any multiplication problems, then the tester knows that Mrs.

Jones's class is having difficulties. Remediation, or correction, is necessary in this classroom.

In OBE, every child must demonstrate compliance with every outcome in the state standard in order to be promoted or to graduate. So the testing *must* be trackable, or there will be no way to know if remediation is working, and children are moving toward the state standard.

State rhetoric about specifics on outcomes and their remediation is fuzzy, so often the most accurate way to know what the state means by such vague language is to look at the tests on the state and local levels. Examination of these tests reveals what is being measured, and when the same kind of question reappears over time, it becomes possible to see what specific attitudes the government is "remediating" toward a state standard.

Values appraisals like those cited in chapter 1 raise serious questions about what the government is attempting to measure and remediate. Because, just as in Mrs. Jones's third grade class, there is no point in testing if there is no action to correct those who did not pass the test.

In classroom activities like the Lifeboat Problem (shown below), a parent needs to ask what is being remediated.

The Lifeboat Problem[7]

A passenger liner is wrecked at sea. *Fifteen* people find themselves together in a lifeboat. Unfortunately, the lifeboat can only support *nine* people. If six people are not eliminated, everyone will die!

Imagine that *you* are in command and *you* must choose the six who will die and the nine who will live.

Here are some details about the people in the lifeboat.

1. A crippled boy, paralyzed since birth. He cannot use his hands and must be fed by others. He can do nothing for himself. Age 8.

2. A doctor. He is nervous because he is a drug addict. Age 60.

3. A married couple. He: construction worker, drinks a lot. Age 27. She: housewife, two children at home. Age 23.

4. A Black minister, Protestant. Age 27.

5. A Jewish restaurant owner, married, two children at home. Age 45.

6. A prostitute, no family. She has previously saved a child from drowning, and is an excellent nurse. Age 36.

7. A teacher, considered the best teacher in his city. Married. Age 32.

8. A criminal, male, charged with murder. He is the only one capable of navigating the boat. Age 37.

9. A Catholic nun. Supervisor of a girl's school. Age 45.

10. A man, mentally disturbed, who carries important U. S. Government secrets in his head. These secrets are vital for defense of the country. Age 42.

11. A beggar. Formerly a professor of literature. He has a great sense of humor, showed courage in the last war, spent three years in a concentration camp, and is now getting his life back together. Age 42.

12. A salesman. Sells automatic washers, and is a member of the American Legion. Unmarried. Age 51.

13. A young couple, married and deeply in love, no children yet. Both citizens of China. He: studying to be a pharmacist. She: housewife, helps with kindergarten. Ages: 24.

INSTRUCTIONS: 1. Make a list of the people that you would save. 2. Make a list of the people that you would cast into the sea to die. 3. Give a reason why you would condemn or save each person.

Many assessments, like this one, create a universe of choices that force youngsters to change personal values. In this case, they are instructed to choose murder. Why throw anyone overboard? Instead, shouldn't children think of solutions to save everyone—such as having passengers swim in hour shifts?

It is important to remember that OBE is an assessment-driven system in which every piece of the curriculum must be tied to an outcome and able to be measured by an assessment.

What desirable outcome could possibly be achieved through an activity like the lifeboat problem?

Assessment is the key to OBE, because whoever controls the test automatically sets the standards and controls the direction of the curriculum. And the state controls the test.

Total Control

OBE states will go one step further. They will forbid outside testing. The only test allowed will be the state-controlled assessment.

As an educational practice this is unsound. It means that the system is only measured against itself. There are no independent appraisals, or reality checks, to verify whether the OBE system works.

In fact, it doesn't work. In Kentucky, the district with the greatest number of Merit Scholars, college-bound graduates, and highest SAT scores did poorly on the state OBE test. Generally, the poorest districts in Appalachian Kentucky scored better on the state test than the western Kentucky districts.

But, instead of questioning the reliability of the state scores, which flew in the face of every other objective measurement of school achievement, Kentucky is ordering the western districts to change their curricula to improve their state assessment test scores.

From a parent's point of view, this is outrageous. Children are being given tests, which no one can see, scored on their responses, and remediated toward the state-desired response. Teachers and schools are evaluated on their demonstrated improvement in having children reach the state standards on the state assessments. And, states are stripping any outside academic measuring instruments from the realms of their schools so their definition of "successful OBE" will be irrefutable.

In the OBE school bus, the state is in the driver's seat. Parents: do you know where the state is taking your children? Do you approve?

Endnotes

1. *Pennsylvania Student Questionnaire*, Grade 8, Pennsylvania Department of Education, n.d., 21, Pennsylvania Education Quality Assessment test. (see chapter 7)

2. High School Level Part I Reading and Mathematics, Pennsylvania System of School Assessment, Pennsylvania Department of Education (1994): 3.

3. George F. Madaus and Thomas Kellaghan, "The British Experience with 'Authentic' Testing," *Phi Delta Kappan* (February 1993): 458-469.

4. Associated Press, "Rand Study Points to Problems In Vermont's Portfolio Assessment Program," *The Executive Educator* (February 1993): 6.

5. Student Test Booklet, Form 2, Grade 8, Kentucky Department of Education (1991-1992): Page 38.

6. Kansas Reading and Mathematics Assessment, Middle/Jr. High, Form D4 (1993): 7.

7. Lifeboat Problem, 11th Grade English, Extra Credit. Carrick High School, Pittsburgh, Pennsylvania (March 1994).

FOUR

THE MARRIAGE OF BUSINESS AND EDUCATION

Below Big Brother was the elite Inner Party. The Outer Party was the dumb masses, numbering eighty-five per cent of the population. "Admission to either branch of the Party is by examination, taken at the age of sixteen."
—George Orwell, *1984*

"Graduation" OBE Style

Connie Chung's TV crew focuses cameras on America's first Certificate of Initial Mastery (CIM) "graduation" ceremony. High school *sophomores* parade across Oregon's Cottage Grove High School stage to receive their certificates. On this historic, sunny, 1994 June morning, outcome-based education's new "diploma" becomes a reality.

Cottage Grove's principal glows with pride as he tells the TV crew, "Not only are children being taught the basics, but they are required to apply them in practical ways."[1]

Earlier that morning, cameras captured another press conference. About one hundred adults and several CIM students were protesting. Nicole Doggett stated that as a student in CIM's pilot outcome-based education program, she had hoped to get a quality education. But, she said, "I find it difficult to be proud of this piece of paper because I did not receive the education I deserved." Nicole added she wished she had attended a different school with traditional teaching.[2] Many dissatisfied pupils did transfer out of this CIM school.

Another student told reporters that, although outcome skills sound good, they're "hung up on political correctness." The teenager added that fundamentals such as reading and writing were no longer taught. Content was left out. This pupil quoted one teacher who said he was now teaching students only one-fourth of his normal curriculum.[3]

Similar to many OBE schools, students' grades were *A*, *B*, or *I* (*In progress*). In fact, although about one hundred sophomores received their CIM, seventy-five others were still "In progress." And, a few youngsters hadn't completed the thirty hours of community service required for graduation.

Although Janice Kincaid's daughter, Karen, received a CIM, Janice wasn't impressed. Her daughter had a 4.0 (straight *A*) average. "This new education is supposed to better prepare students for the work force. But does it prepare them for college?" asks Janice. "My daughter didn't even know Abraham Lincoln freed the slaves."[4]

CIM = OBE's "Diploma"

An *Education Week* headline in 1991 warned, "Oregon Bill Would End Traditional Schooling After the Tenth Grade."[5] But, most parents, like Janice, felt unprepared for its reality. Before this Workstart education bill passed, astute legislators had fought it. They believed schools should not march to the orders of the elite in business and labor. Some legislators called the work force education law, "Big Brother Orwellian." By 1997, law requires all Oregon schools to mandate the Certificate of Initial Mastery.

"That's Oregon. It will never happen in my state," you say.

That's what parents of children in Massachusetts and Washington said. (Those states already mandate the certificate, a new work force "diploma," for graduation.) *Convince* the parents in Alaska, Alabama, Maine, New York, Pennsylvania, Mississippi, Kansas, Indiana, and other states considering this new certificate. *Prove* that the CIM isn't knocking on their schoolhouse doors.[6]

OBE's revolving school door throws four years of required high school out, then ushers in the CIM. *Education Week* says the CIM will "supersede" the high school diploma.[7] Ernest L. Boyer, president of the Carnegie Foundation, told *New York Times*, "I am among the first to say the time has come to abolish it [Carnegie Units]."[8] Of course Boyer wants to dump graduation requirements. William Spady quoted him extensively in a grant proposal to put outcome-based education in all American schools.

This mid-1980s proposal cites Boyer as saying the last two years of high school should be considered a " 'transition school' program."[9] According to this OBE blueprint, school will begin at age four, so by age sixteen, children can engage in "service and work study programs."[10] Business demands a work force, "hands-on" education, not more English or math. That's why OBE's plan is to channel students, after age sixteen, away from academics and into apprenticeships. The CIM will end traditional schooling at about age sixteen, or after tenth grade.[11]

Business is also requiring student attitudes to conform. To properly groom industry's international worker, his thoughts must fit into a global mold. Rather than a diploma proving you've completed four years of high school, the CIM certifies you've mastered outcomes—few of them academic—many politically correct. One Oregon parent observes, "We're watching a transfer from the three R's to the four G's—grade inflation, green peace, group cooperation and global awareness."

Work Force Track

Many fear the CIM will "track" young people into career choices too early. How might early tracking affect a bright child who is a "late bloomer"? Germany uses a similar system. At the end of sixth grade, teachers recommend each student go into either an apprenticeship or a university track.[12] China and the former USSR also use educational tracking.

In fact, the 1984 Soviet education reform law for the twenty-first century required schools to ensure "participation of the schoolchildren in . . . productive labor."[13] It mandated that students acquire a trade while in school. The law also shortened compulsory education from ten years to nine and lowered school entrance age from seven to six. Children could now begin a university track or exit into labor two years earlier.

Ninth grade became the threshold at which selection took place—the majority of fifteen-year-olds now joined the work force. In 1950, 80 percent of Soviet children entered an institution of higher education. That figure continued to drop to less than 18 percent.[14] The Soviet state discovered its greatest need was not for well-educated students, but for willing workers. Did this 1984 Soviet reform improve academics? According to a research professor from the former USSR Academy of Science, "The 1984 reform totally destroyed our schools."[15]

In preparation for CIM's two-track system for sixteen-year-olds, all OBE schools must eventually eliminate the "general education" track. Many outcome-based education schools have already done this. Students now must choose between a college-prep or technical-prep track. One problem with the death of the general track is that children may be locked into a career decision too early in life.

Although business may think this is a good idea, do you? Did you know what you wanted to be by tenth grade? America's unique education with its general track offers students a broad education. Has our system of allowing children to decide careers at an older age diminished, for example, our pool of scientists? Interestingly, America's number of doctorates in engineering and physical science is at an all-time high.[16]

CIM = Work Force Diploma

In Oregon, the general track has been eliminated. After getting the CIM, students choose among six occupational paths. Some high schoolers then receive a new set of outcomes toward their Certificate of Advanced Mastery (CAM).

All students begin apprenticeships (this sheds new light on OBE's rhetoric that students must demonstrate what they know and can do—literally).

The CIM diploma will affect a student's getting hired or going to college. One draft of Oregon's law made it *illegal* for employers to hire anyone under eighteen without the CIM, or for any public college to enroll an Oregon student "who has not obtained a Certificate of Initial Mastery."[17]

Both prohibiting employers from hiring and forbidding public institutions from admitting students without a CIM were spelled out in Oregon's original bill. Although modified in the final draft, the intent of CIM's control is clear.

Washington, another OBE pilot, recommends that students under eighteen without a Certificate of Mastery and who are not in public school should not be hired.

National Education Association—
OBE Cheerleaders

No cheerleaders could be more enthusiastic about OBE with its new diploma than big business and labor. The nation's largest labor union is the teachers' National Education Association (NEA). In fact, in 1993, the NEA publicly announced its intention "to disseminate information about OBE through membership publications."[18] Three major factors drive this labor union to wholehearted support of outcome-based education with its CIM.

First, OBE's politically correct outcomes are an overlay of the NEA's left-wing political agenda. So, it feeds mountains of pro-OBE information to its 2.1 million members. And, it actively fights those opposing OBE. Nebraska's NEA raised dues by four dollars to "combat the darkest threat in the history of public education" (groups opposing OBE).[19]

Second, OBE reform promises the NEA power through site-based management. Usurping power from the elected school boards, each school develops site-councils (called site-based management, school council, etc.). Although comprised of community members, the majority of voting members are usually teachers who are union members.

Third, as the NEA's political clout expands, its drive to improve academic education diminishes. *Forbes* points out that this union's growing power "is directly linked with the thirty-year decline of American education that occurred simultaneously."[20] Changing education's goal from traditional education to a school-to-work education, hides NEA's failure to improve academics.

OBE's theme, "All students shall succeed," pressures teachers to inflate grades and slash standards. Self-esteem and anti-biased attitudes become academic subjects. It's an excuse to replace standardized tests with new assessments, proving OBE works. For example, the Scholastic Aptitude Test [SAT] was changed to the Scholastic Assessment Test [SAT] to line up with education's new outcome-based thrust. A student who scored a 420 (out of 800) in "verbal" will now receive a 500 under the new system.[21]

Thomas Sowell's acclaimed education expose, *Inside American Education* says these two trends—grade inflation and declining SAT scores—are by no means unconnected. The author calls this a "systematic deception of parents and the public."[22]

U.S. Government: OBE Cheerleader

Labor's government arm, the U.S. Department of Labor, is for the first time fueling an education issue. OBE is a marriage. The U.S. Department of Labor joined the U.S. Department of Education and gave birth to "reinventing K-12 education."

The reinvented American school focuses on achieving work force outcomes. The Department of Labor's *SCANS* (Secretary's Commission on Achieving Necessary Skills) report also tells schools to "reinvent" themselves around one "universally" recognized standard—a Certificate of Initial Mastery.

In fact, *SCANS* decrees that it is society's "obligation" to provide opportunities for every student to obtain the CIM.[23] You may say, "Let labor make demands, educators won't pay attention. Isn't *SCANS* just another obscure manual pumped out by the federal government?" Unfortunately, everybody's treating it as if it were federal *law*. Education periodicals call it "the most important document to come out of the federal government since the Bill of Rights."[24]

The *SCANS* Scam

Across the nation, all states are falling under the spell of the *SCANS* report. From Florida, where two million students adopted its skills (outcomes),[25] to Wisconsin, where their statewide outcomes were "adapted" from the *SCANS* report.[26]

What are some of the Labor Department skills/outcomes being used? *SCANS* lists: sociability, mental visualization, responsibility, decision-making, works with cultural diversity. Although laudable, and worthy to be modeled by teachers, these outcomes are not appropriate to teach and grade. A report card in one Wisconsin OBE school grades students on whether or not they "will project anti-racist, anti-biased attitudes."[27]

What do grassroots folks think about trading traditional learning for this kind of work-oriented, behavior-modifying schooling? When a group of anti-OBE Pennsylvania parents obtained a copy of the *SCANS* report from the federal government, they were shocked. They had assumed Pennsylvania's OBE push was from their state's department of education. Now, they saw OBE's source was federal, the U.S. Department of Labor.

These parents discovered that *SCANS* talked about making the proper worker for tomorrow. And, children were referred to as "human resources"[28]—like coal or trees, objects used as raw material to fuel a nation's economy.

The group remembered how educators had often explained to the press, "Outcome-based education is not about what the schools will teach, but what the student will demonstrate." With tongue in cheek, to illustrate that concept, parents used as an outcome, honesty. "Even if it's a value we agree on, like honesty, should the state be given authority to set a standard for honesty?" Then, parents would ask, "Will the state test our youngster's integrity? And, will it deny him or her a job because our child didn't meet the state's honesty standard?" It was a joke, an absurd example to make a point.

Yet, on page sixty-five in the *SCANS* report, they found an "honesty" standard. A hypothetical resumé for Jane Smith (age nineteen) showed her grade for honesty. The resumé listed Jane's Workplace Competency Skills, Academics Courses, and *Personality Qualities*. Evidently this resumé was the prototype all schools were supposed to use: a new exit "report card."

Each category displayed the level of proficiency she mastered. In "honesty," Jane only received a "6." But, in sociability and self-esteem, Jane scored a perfect "10."[29] "How sociable must a high school student be? My teenager's sociability goes up and down like a yo-yo, depending on who asked her for a date," commented one mother. "What employer," the Pennsylvania parents wondered, "would hire a self-confident extrovert with a '6' in honesty?"

On the page opposite Jane's resumé, the parents read, "Most students will earn their certificate of initial mastery [CIM] by age 16, but no age limit should be imposed."[30] Jane Smith, according to her resumé had only earned three hundred points toward her CIM, but five hundred were required. Unbelievably, Jane, at age nineteen, was still in tenth grade. Why did *SCANS* use such a negative example? Does Jane's low score imply most students will need reeducation in attitudes? What message is the Department of Labor's *SCANS* giving Americans?

Labor's Curriculum

This *SCANS* resumé raises other troubling questions. Since business insists that "Personal Qualities" actually be taught, tested, and scored, will results be sent to future employers? How will a student be tested and retested until that child gets "honesty" right? Jane was denied her CIM; without it could she get a job?

States like Oregon are telling their schools to use *SCANS* skills. Keep in mind that it is the outcomes that drive the curriculum and states' outcomes, are based on *SCANS* "competencies." That's why the U.S. Labor Department is actually suggesting schools use a curriculum called "SCANS Full Curriculum." How academic is it? The curriculum itself says 33 percent of its test assesses values and attitudes.[31]

Ohio's Mayfield City School District integrated the *SCANS* curriculum along with the International Baccalaureate Degree in grades nine through twelve. Just as the *SCANS* resumé of Jane Smith reveals, one curriculum section tests Personality Qualities. Skills tested are ranked by level of difficulty: low is (1), moderate is (2), and high is (3):

Level of Difficulty	Skills Tested
(3)	"Demonstrate enthusiasm/vitality/optimism in approaching tasks."
(2)	"Express empathy for others."
(3)	"Respond to feedback unemotionally and non-defensively."[32]

How will these new work force "skills" be taught, tested, remediated, and retested? The school is supposed to mold, then test personality qualities. Labor's *SCANS* modestly recommends, "The nation's school system should make the *SCANS* foundational skills and workplace competencies explicit objectives of instruction at all levels."[33]

Business Goes to School

SCANS enthusiastically quotes the Business Roundtable agenda for schools. This powerful organization, made up of CEOs from some of the nation's largest corporations, created a nine-point education reform. Of course, it includes an outcome-based system. Senior advisor, David Hornbeck, travels nationwide promoting its radical "reform."

Hornbeck sells legislators on business' nine-point education agenda, such as pre-kindergarten, health and social services in schools, an advocate for every child, site-based management, education based on outcomes, etc. Each item must be used "to delete any one principle is to flaw the entire effort."[34] These nine elements ensure that all "human capital," from cradle to grave, will conform to business/ government needs.

What is the parent's role in this picture? Why must all youngsters have an adult advocate? Why should every school have a health-based clinic? Doesn't business trust parents with its human resources? Why make schools a "nanny"? Who owns the children?

A book Hornbeck helped write captures the Roundtable's social agenda for schools: "What is essential is that we create a seamless web of opportunities to develop one's skills that literally extends from cradle to grave . . . regulated on the basis of outcomes."[35]

The Business Roundtable also promotes school/business partnerships. The school/business partnership in Mercer County, Pennsylvania, locks Timothy out of the job of his choice. Timothy's OBE school offers a school/business partnership card, based on attendance and citizenship. Even with an *A* average, Tim is refused work because he doesn't want to apply for a card. At a large shoe store, he was told by the manager, "Don't apply. Only students who have cards will be considered for work." For other jobs, Help Wanted ads state: "Proof of membership in School/Business Partnership required."[36] Without that card, top students like Tim are locked out of some jobs.

Concerns

Business involvement in curriculum change remains very controversial. Educators worry that business and labor may emphasize job-specific courses. Will hands-on learning take time from studying the Constitution and reading Shakespeare?

The more control business acquires over school, the more influence it will have over curriculum. Business needs human resource materials (students) that best fit its self-interests. The CIM suits these needs well. However, many educators fear this new system might push students not bound for college into blue-collar jobs too early.

America's Choice—
Business/Education Road Map

Labor and business relied heavily on one key report, *America's Choice: high skills or low wages!*, published in 1990 by the National Center on Education and the Economy (notice the name relates education to economy). *America's Choice* unveiled a road map showing how to reinvent America's schools. No one asked if this map would take students in a dangerous direction. Instead, Labor's *SCANS*, federal laws like GOALS 2000, and state legislation, such as Oregon's education act, followed it—blindly.

Yet, *America's Choice* was based on a false assumption. Its chairman, a social planner named Ira Magaziner, also co-promoted the controversial nationalized health-care package. Many of Magaziner's projects experienced a history of failure. This study set out to prove that business and labor desperately needed schools to produce droves of skilled workers. But, according to the progressive publication, *The New Republic*, "Magaziner discovered that most executives didn't think they suffered from a skills shortage."[37]

Did Magaziner admit education didn't need to be reinvented? No. The intricate plan to place schools into the hands of industry was too important. *The New Republic's* article, "Dies Ira: The Dismal Track Record of Ira Magaziner," sarcastically observes that finding no skill scarcity "didn't dampen his enthusiasm for designing another plan."[38] What was his other plan? Simple. Market the idea of turning schools into work force factories by redefining the word *skills*.

New Skills = Attitudes

In his National Center report, Magaziner redefines *skill* to mean "social behavior."[39] *America's Choice* contends business' primary concern is not in finding good readers, but workers with "appropriate social behavior: 'reliable,' 'a good attitude,' 'a pleasant appearance,' 'a good personality.' "[40] This explains why *SCANS* won't let Jane Smith out of school until she masters state-mandated attitudes. To emphasize its new definition of skills, *America's Choice* says this nation's greatest challenge is "to instill in our youth the *attitude* and *social manners* required for work in an advanced industrial nation" (emphasis added).[41]

As you see, the bull's-eye toward which this world-class education is aiming is training students in attitudes, not academics. That's the justification for outcome-based education. It reeducates students until they get outcomes—such as cooperating with others—right. Creating "good personalities" (not better thinkers) with "approved attitudes" (not more knowledge) is the rationale behind why assessment tests measure attitudes.

Who defines what is a "good personality"? Is it an extrovert or an introvert? A good talker or a good listener?

Looking at *America's Choice*

America's Choice is affecting much more than the redefinition of skills. The manual has been so influential, it requires a closer look. *America's Choice* highlights a Certificate of Initial Mastery and says that youngsters who will not, or cannot, pass the CIM test will be referred to newly created youth centers.[42] According to the report, "ideally there would be a Youth Center in every community or neighborhood."[43] Open year-round, the centers should provide basic education, plus a full range of health and social services. Today, these youth centers are called by various names: Family Resource Centers (Iowa and Kentucky), Learning Centers (Oregon), Family Centers (Pennsylvania). Today, they're up and running—ready for full implementation of this plan.

"Once Youth Centers are established, we propose that the child labor laws be amended," states this heavy-handed report. And, new laws must grant work permits only to youths up to age eighteen who have a CIM.[44] (You can see where Oregon and Washington got their idea.) Why pass legislation making it impossible for high schoolers to hold part-time jobs? Doesn't working for pay teach a child "real life education" and make education relevant? Isn't forcing new laws that require a CIM as a prerequisite for employment coercive? The document candidly admits this may seem "draconian."[45]

Its section on lifelong learning raises more questions. Eventually, must *all* citizens earn a CIM to be hired? *America's Choice's* flow charts indicate adult workers may have to move down the career ladder and obtain a CIM before they can progress back up.

Interestingly, every OBE school, either in a mission statement or in outcomes, includes the term "lifelong learning." When one parent asked what it meant, he was told, "Look the definition up in a dictionary." Most citizens assume lifelong learning means reading books or taking golf lessons as you age, not an intrusive state-mandated certification program.

But, *America's Choice* makes the definition clearer. In a chapter entitled "Lifelong Learning," the manual talks about yearly recertification for adults.[46] Will required "state education" be expanded over one's entire life? Will choosing to stay home with your children qualify you as a "lifelong learner"? In China, "lifelong learning" means citizens attend political indoctrination meetings weekly.

False Assumptions

America's Choice bases its sweeping reforms on the presupposition that businesses are crying for better skilled workers. This is given as the reason for business and labor to aggressively takeover the direction of classroom instruction. Preparing students for the work force is the major excuse OBE uses for getting away from "seat time" and making its outcomes "relevant" to "real life problems."

But, the fact remains, OBE is based on a false assumption. As mentioned, *The New Republic* reported most executives did not believe they experienced a lack of skilled workers. Even *America's Choice* itself admits only 5 percent of employees believe a work skills shortage exists.[47]

Marketing *America's Choice*

Yet, this document is key in getting an overview of an important piece of OBE's complicated plan. As the *Rich-*

mond Times-Dispatch points out, "Ira [Magaziner] and Hillary [Clinton] really got the ball rolling for OBE" with *America's Choice*.[48]

Work force education with its CIM centerpiece has been aggressively marketed. Interestingly, the National Center paid one of its then board members, Hillary Rodham Clinton, $101,630 to peddle the CIM.[49] In 1991, Ms. Clinton praised Oregon's "Workstart" education bill for using *America's Choice*. She also said that Oregon's bill may play a "key role" in influencing the school-to-work debate nationally.[50] It has. As previously mentioned, Massachusetts and other states used it as a blueprint for their radical reforms.

Oregon: A Model for America

Federal incentives will most likely tempt your state to launch similar OBE-style legislation. That's why Oregon's bill is being examined. Various states' OBE/restructuring mandates resemble making a cake: Some cakes are made from complete mixes (like bills in Oregon, Massachusetts, Missouri, Kentucky, etc.); others are the result of adding eggs, sugar, and flour separately (like mandates in Pennsylvania, Kansas, Florida, Colorado, etc.). Once removed from the oven, however, all cakes will look the same.

To pass its "Workstart" Education Act, Oregon declared an emergency on 1 July 1991: "This Act being necessary for the immediate preservation of the public peace, health and safety, an emergency is declared to exist."[51] A state of emergency preempts public rights.

But, Oregon's massive law passed with no appropriations. Many citizens hope that a lack of funds will handcuff implementation. After all, its estimated cost is $2.5 billion.[52] Three years later, President Clinton's radical education bills (i.e. GOALS 2000) promised federal funding to states doing OBE-style reform. Locking states into federal money was expected by change agents in Oregon who pushed this outcome-based education reform.[53]

Mandating OBE

Following the *SCANS* guidelines, children's attitudes will be assessed. A report interpreting Oregon's bill says, "Qualities such as responsibility, self-esteem, social skills, and integrity apply to the development of all the CIM outcomes."[54] In 1993, one pilot CIM high school told students to write what their values were—"a good family life, a clean environment, conformity, power, etc." This "Values Activity Sheet" required students' names. Other values appraisals given in the same CIM school included: "I read the Bible or other religious writing regularly," "I love my parents."

Will the law mandate OBE? A brochure explaining Oregon's act clearly states, "All educators will provide outcome-based education."[55] However, the outcomes won't be revealed until after the law is passed—when no elected body will approve them. Three years after the law passed, a 1994 survey shows the majority of Oregon's citizens still haven't heard of outcome-based education. A mere sixteen out of every hundred citizens approve of OBE.[56]

Tracking in Career Paths

As discussed earlier, the Oregon act also establishes a Certificate of Initial Mastery (of OBE's outcomes), which all students by about age sixteen will have to pass. Then, youngsters will be tracked into a vocational or professional career. A *Newsweek* article on Oregon's bill says critics attacked this new "tracking system" as "undemocratic."[57]

Yet, students unable or unwilling to merit a CIM will be referred to learning centers. There the student will be monitored intensively, even if he/she moves.

The bill states that "adults who wish to pursue a Certificate of Initial Mastery may also attend a Learning Center." Just as in *Americas' Choice*, Oregon's act encourages centers to become one-stop social services for adult and youths by including the following: day care, after school child care, health services, family crisis and mental health counseling.

Who Owns the Children?

Oregon's bill warns, "If, at any point, a student is not making satisfactory progress toward . . . the Certificate of Initial Mastery," school services include "family evaluation."[58]

Who owns the child—school or parent? In 1993, Oregon passed a law threatening to fine parents one hundred dollars if their child skips school.[59]

The education act also proposes integrating "health and social services at the school site." Will school-based clinics offer birth control or abortion without parents' knowledge? A list of "Benchmarks" for schools includes: "The birth rate will not exceed four per 1,000 females ages 10-17." And, "98 percent of babies will be at healthy birthweight."[60]

If a pregnant student is a collaborative learner, might she consider abortion to help her school reach the state's benchmarks? How might a female deal with pressure to "Understand Positive Health Habits"—one of the CIM outcomes?

Work Force Education

Oregon's bill establishes partnership among business, labor, schools, and on-the-job training and apprenticeships. A task force report says that Oregonians "must recognize integration of the workplace and classroom is a necessity."[61] Is school focus being redirected from academics to the work force? Will apprenticeships be required of all students?

This task force report continues, "Remember that the employer is both a *customer* and a partner in this effort" (emphasis added).[62] Citizens wonder who made business a customer? If parents now must share customer status, which patron will schools please? Are schools reinventing themselves to please business, not parents?

Labor's School Government

Is labor (NEA) also taking control from parents? Oregon's bill states that each school is required to have an appointed Twenty-First Century School Council (building site committee). The act gives labor control. The majority of this building site committee "shall be active classroom teachers." Union members are given unheard-of authority to preempt the elected school board. If site committee decisions "conflict with a recommendation of the local school committee, the decision of the building site committee shall prevail."[63]

In other words, teachers (NEA, labor union) will now control curriculum and policy in the school building. All three—labor's *SCANS*, Business' Roundtable, and tax-exempt foundations' *America's Choice*—blueprint site committee management. Even the *Washington Post* warns "outcome-based education would restrict the power of local school boards."[64] It's a dangerous power shift from elected representatives—local school boards—to NEA union control.

If It Ain't Broke, Why Fix It?

Whether in Oregon or your state, this marriage of education with business is an unholy union. Students don't exist for the government or business. Government schools have forgotten that in America the government is of the people, by the people, and for the people.

The U.S. traditional high school is uniquely American. Should we break its mold to suit the needs of business? After all, when the brightest students from around the world come to American universities, our students experience no difficulty competing. Since the 1950s, Americans have won more Nobel Prizes than all other nations combined.[65] Why reinvent education?

Social planners in business and labor use the excuse that we must prepare students for a rapidly changing world with a new service-oriented economy. They say that "industrial age" education is a broken antique. Only OBE can adequately offer a twenty-first century, world-class education.

To sell world-class education, OBE promoters use a technique we mentioned earlier, called mnemonics. In Aldous Huxley's *Brave New World*, a novel about a futuristic collective society, the masses are controlled by mnemonic phrases called *hypnopedia*—mindless phrases repeated so often that they become "truth." OBE change agents repeatedly say traditional education is industrial-age education (negative) and OBE is twenty-first century, world-class education (positive).

The *New York Times* points out that OBE has the rhetoric "down pat." However, while other industrial nations call for skills like solving linear equations, OBE promoters repeat the phrase "world-class standards" but mean outcomes like "maintain emotional and social well-being."[66]

OBE's slogans may sound convincing. But, didn't traditional education adequately prepare our grandparents to overcome rapid change (economic depression, global wars)? They experienced exploding knowledge (from ink wells to word processors, from biplanes to space travel). Didn't America's traditional three Rs equip grandparents to think critically and to solve problems? What made America the leading nation in a rapidly changing world—OBE's twenty-first century, world-class education or the three Rs' industrial-age education?

Why risk destroying schools (and a generation of children) for a phony bill of goods? The reasoning is as nonsensical as OBE's vacuous mnemonic slogans. Yet, OBE's shadow advances across America, swiftly.

Meet the Players

NEA is delighted. It gets more power through site-based management; new assessment tests to hide watered-down academics; and behavior-changing outcomes to mold children.

Federal government is thrilled. NEA's huge lobby expresses gratitude with financial contributions and political favors; the U.S. Department of Labor reinvents education; and federal bills extend government control into states.

Big business is self-satisfied. Schools are an untapped marketplace (e.g., computer company sales will skyrocket with technology as a mandated outcome); school apprenticeships supply free workers; future employees will work anywhere or with anyone; workers will accept wages and working conditions—without protest.

Tax-exempt foundations (funding organizations, like the National Center) are pleased. Their long-planned, liberal agenda for utilizing American schools appears unstoppable.

It's a collaboration of Big Labor, Big Government, Big Education, Big Business. Their goal? To produce students who will *know, do,* and *be like* what government/business wants.

Redefining Who's Literate

Remember that *America's Choice* revealed business doesn't believe more skilled workers are needed? So the word *skill* was redefined to mean—not reading or computing—but "social behavior." OBE also redefines *literacy*.

OBE promoters say because the twenty-first century will demand a more highly skilled work force, *literacy* must mean "much more than the three R's."[67] Rather than reading books, literacy now includes, "appreciate differences in belief systems," and the "ability to live in one world as one community of nations."[68] An OBE school in Wisconsin has a report card that grades students on demonstrating an "understanding of global interdependence."[69]

To become a marketable, literate student, your child will find his toughest academic course will be *citizenship*. According to a pro-OBE article, "Of all the educational objectives, good citizenship may be the most difficult."[70] Yet, your youngster will not have to learn more about the Constitution and Civil War battles—those "old" academics aren't mentioned. Good citizenship isn't what a student must *know.* Passing the *citizenship* outcome is determined by what a student is able *to do* and *be like.*

Effective School Report explains that increased global interdependency "will require that all citizens become better citizens." How must your child become a better citizen? By doing mandated community service. The article says, "Community service is recognized as a necessary learning option."[71]

One national OBE break-the-mold school called Odyssey, which big business funded, required 220 hours of community service for students and 20 hours for parents.[72] Tulsa, Oklahoma, tried to pass a regulation suggesting 10 hours of voluntary service from parents.[73] Today, in Maryland, all students must spend 75 hours in community service to graduate.

And, usually volunteer hours spent doing church-related or politically conservative projects aren't acceptable. Community service is defined as "not associated with the practice or promotion of any specific religion" in Massachusetts' Concord-Carlisle Regional High *Community Service Handbook*.[74]

OBE School Says, "No Diploma!"

Since citizenship is an outcome, will students get a Certificate of Mastery so they can move into work or enter higher education only if they *do* (demonstrate) citizenship? Today schools are actually enforcing mandatory "voluntary" service to get a high school diploma. Consider the story of David Moralis:

On his graduation invitation card, "YOU ARE CORDIALLY INVITED" appears under a picture of deflated, sad, gray balloons. Inside, the message continues, "TO ATTEND AN ALTERNATIVE GRADUATION FOR THE SENIORS OF LIBERTY AND FREEDOM WHO ARE DENIED THEIR DIPLOMA FOR FAILURE TO COMPLETE THE MANDATORY COMMUNITY SERVITUDE REQUIREMENT. R.S.V.P." On the back appears:

> NEITHER SLAVERY NOR INVOLUNTARY SERVITUDE, EXCEPT AS A PUNISHMENT FOR CRIME . . . , SHALL EXIST WITHIN THE UNITED STATES . . .
> —THIRTEENTH AMENDMENT; SECTION I[75]

America's forefathers outlawed "involuntary servitude" (unpaid, forced service). The Constitution says, except as a punishment for crime, it's illegal.

David Moralis was the ideal American high school student. His grade point average was 3.8 and he blew the top off the Scholastic Aptitude Test (SAT), scoring 780 (out of a possible 800) in math. Although participating in school activities, he found time to read regularly to his blind grandmother. However, that wasn't counted as community service.

David believed mandating volunteerism for graduation was unconstitutional, so he and several of his classmates refused to demonstrate "good citizenship" by completing sixty hours of required "voluntary" community service. In 1994, when his class graduated, David was denied his high school diploma. He isn't the kind of human resource business wants. By OBE's new definition of academics, David isn't literate.

Endnotes

1. Ed Otton, principal, Cottage Grove High School, press statement, Cottage Grove, Oregon, 10 June 1994.

2. Nicole Doggett, student, press statement, Cottage Grove, Oregon, 10 June 1994.

3. Anonymous, student, press statement, Cottage Grove, Oregon, 10 June 1994.

4. Phone interview by author with Janice Kincaid, 8 July 1994.

5. Lonnie Harp, "Ore. Bill Would End Traditional Schooling After the 10th Grade," *Education Week* (15 May 1991): 1, 20.

6. Lynn Olson, "Center Presses 'Certificate of Initial Mastery,'" *Education Week* (20 April 1994): 1, 11.

7. Ibid., 1.

8. Michael deCourcy Hinds, "Where School is More Than Just Showing Up," *New York Times*, 21 July 1994, B10.

9. William G. Spady and Gary Marx, "Excellence in Our Schools: Making it Happen" (American Association of School Administrators and the Far West Laboratory, 1984), 17. (Grant proposal to U. S. Department of Education.)

10. Ibid.

11. Harp, "Ore. Bill Would End,"　1.

12. Bruce Adams, "Apprenticeship Programs in Germany," *Oregon Education* (Dec/Jan 1994): 20.

13. *Pravda* (14 April 1984) as quoted in Mikhail Heller, *Cogs in the Wheel: The Formation of Soviet Man* (New York: Alfred A. Knopf, 1988), 164.

14. *Pravda* (7 January 1984) as quoted in Heller, *Cogs in the Wheel*, 163–164.

15. Personal interview by author with Felix Rizvanov, 12 June 1994.

16. Daniel Tanner, "A Nation 'Truly' At Risk," *Phi Delta Kappan* (December 1993): 293.

17. Oregon Education Act for the 21st Century, 31 July 1991, H.B. 3565, 5. Found in Section 23 (B), Section 25 (1), (2).

18. "NEA New Business Item 15," *Education Reporter* (August 1993): 2.

19. Jack Kennedy, "NSEA Raises Dues To Combat New Right," *Lincoln Journal-Star*, 25 April 1993.

20. Peter Brimelow and Leslie Spencer, "The National Extortion Association?" *Forbes* (7 June 1993): 95.

21. Karen Diegmueller, "S.A.T. To Realign Scores for First Time in Half a Century," *Education Week* (22 June 1994): 3.

22. Thomas Sowell, *Inside American Education: The Decline, the Deception, the Dogma* (New York: The Free Press, Macmillan, Inc., 1993), 2.

23. *Learning A Living: A Blueprint for High Performance: A SCANS Report for America 2000*, (U. S. Department of Labor, April 1992), 62.

24. Joseph Stinson, "Beyond Shop Talk: Reinventing High School," *Electronic Learning* (February 1994): 21.

25. Ibid.

26. John D. Fortier and James M. Moser, "Measurable Learner Outcomes" (Wisconsin Department of Public Instruction, 28 May 1992), 15.

27. Milwaukee Public Schools, Grand Avenue Middle School, draft report card (1994-1995).

28. *SCANS*, xiii.

29. Ibid., 65.

30. Ibid., 64.

31. "Secretary's Commission On Achieving Necessary Skills (SCANS) Full Curriculum," from *The Mayfield City School District 1991-1992 Complete Report (1991-1992)*, 164.

32. Ibid., 163–174.

33. *SCANS*, xv.

34. "Alabama Gap Analysis: Developing a Blueprint for Education Reform" (n.p., n.d.): 11.

35. Marc Tucker, *A Human Resources Development Plan for the United States* (Rochester, New York: National Center on Education and the Economy, 1992), 2.

36. "Help Wanted," section *The Herald*, 5 May 1993.

37. Jacob Weisberg, "Dies Ira: The Dismal Track Record of Ira Magaziner," *The New Republic* (24 January 1994): 22.

38. Ibid.

39. Ira Magaziner, chair, *America's Choice: high skills or low wages! The Report of the Commission on the Skills of the American Work Force* (Rochester, New York: National Center on Education and the Economy, June 1990), 3.

40. Ibid.

41. Ibid., 28.

42. Ibid., 78.

43. Ibid., 71.

44. Ibid., 73.

45. Ibid.

46. Ibid., 81.

47. Ibid., 3.

48. Robert Holland, "Big Media Slumber Through School Battle," *Richmond Times-Dispatch*, 26 January 1994, A13.

49. Olson, "Center Presses 'Certificate of Initial Mastery,'" 15.

50. Harp, "Ore. Bill Would End," 1.

51. Oregon Education Act, Section 40, 31 July 1991, 18.

52. Barbara Kantrowitz and Pat Wingert, "Putting Value in Diplomas," *Newsweek* (15 July 1991): 62.

53. Phone interview by author with Charles Starr, Oregon state representative, 25 July 1994.

54. "Task Force Reports Summaries" (Oregon Department of Education, December 1992), 10.

55. "Schools for the 21st Century, Toward Implementation of the Oregon Educational Act for the 21st Century" (Oregon Department of Education, n.d.).

56. Survey conducted by State Rep. Charles Starr (Spring 1994). "Do you approve of Outcome-Based Education?" Response: 16.8 percent approve; 33.0 percent disapprove; 51.2 percent no opinion.

57. Kantrowitz and Wingert, "Diplomas," 62.

58. Oregon Education Act, Section 21 (4), (d), 10.

59. Norm Maves Jr., "Your Kid Skips School? $100 Fine May Be Your Lesson," *The Oregonian*, November 1993, A16.

60. "Task Force Reports Summaries," 53.

61. "School-to-Work Task Force Report" (Oregon Department of Education, 4 November 1993), 6.

62. Ibid.

63. Oregon Education Act, Section 34 (6): 16.

64. John Harris, "Wilder Abandons Curriculum Change," *Washington Post*, 16 September 1993, B1.

65. Tanner, "A Nation 'Truly' at Risk," 296.

66. Albert Shanker, "Outrageous Outcomes," *New York Times*, 12 September 1993, 7.

67. Don Thomas, "Education 90—A Framework for the Future," *The Effective School Report* (September 1990): 1.

68. Ibid.

69. Milwaukee Public Schools, Grand Avenue Middle School, draft report card (1994–1995).

70. Thomas, "Education 90," 3.

71. Ibid.

72. *The Odyssey Project, A Proposal Submitted to New American Schools Development Corporation*, (12 February 1992): 16, 18.

73. Michelle Stevens, "High Schools Teach Wrong Lesson" *Chicago Sun-Times*, 25 April 1994.

74. *Community Service Handbook*, Concord-Carlisle Regional High School (1993-1994), 6.

75. Graduation invitation received by author, 27 May 1994.

FIVE

How Do You Spell School? S-T-A-T-E

The possibility of enforcing not only complete obedience to the will of the State, but complete uniformity of opinion on all subjects, now existed for the first time.
—George Orwell, *1984*

1600 Bills Wink at the Tenth Amendment

Your child may be the next David Moralis. "Not in a free country," you say. But, did you know that America has eight national educational goals, which are now the law of the land? According to federal law, goal number three mandates, "All students will be involved in activities that promote and demonstrate good citizenship, good health, community service, and personal responsibility."[1]

Are you thinking, "It doesn't mention mandating community service"? Doesn't it? Read it again: "*all* students *will* be involved in . . . community service."

Did you know that the federal government recently decreed that citizenship would be an academic subject? In fact, during President Clinton's tenure, an avalanche of education bills—more than sixteen hundred—has snowballed across U.S. legislators' desks.[2] They ranged from the heavy-hitting GOALS 2000: Educate America Act to the flighty-sounding Midnight Basketball League Training and Partnership Act.

But, whether it's Midnight Basketball, which requires each player to attend educational classes immediately following the games,[3] or GOALS 2000, which carves eight national goals into stone, why didn't more media scream, "This is unconstitutional!"? Nationalization of learning opens a door to danger.

Didn't congressional officials take an oath to uphold the Tenth Amendment? That amendment states federal involvement in local education is *verboten*—illegal.[4] The Tenth Amendment reminds them, "The powers not delegated to the United States by the Constitution . . . are reserved to the states."

This is as legally binding as the First Amendment. The government cannot shut down a newspaper or church; neither should federal intrusion in education be tolerated.

In spite of America's Constitution, that avalanche of national education bills attempted to bury local school autonomy forever. "Within a decade we have gone from this preoccupation of local control to national standards," says Ernest L. Boyer, president of the Carnegie Foundation for the Advancement of Teaching.[5] "There is no turning back." He's right. Americans do have a preoccupation with local control; it's a safeguard against nationalism/socialism.

The *New York Times* reported on 30 March 1994, "The nation will for the first time have a federal blueprint to educate its children."[6] Do you want a federal blueprint? Uncle Sam's difficulty in delivering mail and inability to balance the nation's budget give cartoonists great pleasure. Why would you want his clumsy, federal fingers directing your state's education policies—to say nothing of allowing government bureaucrats to dictate what your youngster should read or be taught in her classroom.

But, it won't matter if you don't like the idea. All states, all classrooms will have to join in lock-step, eventually. At least that's what Diane Ravitch, an assistant secretary of education in the Bush administration, wrote in the 26 May 1993 *New York Times*. She said that you do not have to be a "seer" to predict that federal education's new standards would permit federal regulation of 1) curriculum, 2) textbooks, 3) facilities, and 4) instructional methods.[7] She is saying that the federal government will be regulating your child's textbooks, his tests, his curriculum. Obviously Ravitch believes that when bill sponsors talk of "voluntary" standards, they have their fingers crossed. She isn't alone.

New Hampshire's Sen. Judd Gregg points out that, for the first time in our history, the federal bureaucracy will define how education will be delivered on every main street.[8]

Federal Caretaker

Cruising along Main Street, USA, you'll find bright potted flowers lining the street. Under the proud and loving care of local merchants they thrive. However, if left to the care of a distant mall owner who knows nothing about the local climate, nor of the specific needs of each plant, they will wither. American schools do not need a distant caretaker.

Since Massachusetts founded the nation's first public school 150 years ago, education has been well cared for locally. The U.S. education system was built upon the foundation of local control, state influence, and federal interest.[9] That sequence is very important: 1. local (control); 2. state (influence); 3. federal (interest); not the reverse. And, that formula works for both flowers and children. Contrary to the "nation at risk" report, consider what local control has meant for our schools:[10]

  • Since the 1970s, ethnic and racial groups have maintained or improved on SAT (Scholastic Aptitude Test) scores.

  • High school dropout rates are declining for most ethnic populations.

  • Performance on tests for the National Assessment of Educational Progress has been improving.

  • Since the 1970s, Graduate Record Examination scores have risen significantly.

  • The U. S. leads the world in the proportion of its population earning the bachelor's degree—especially in science and engineering.

In 1787, when a draft of the Constitution was presented to America's newly formed independent states, it created substantial federal power. Therefore, the fledgling Congress wisely adopted the amendments called the Bill of Rights. These amendments were to ensure that good intentions did not lead to repressive manipulation.

Prior to 1933, the German public schools were administrated on the local level, and universities were controlled by local states. Soon after Hitler created a Reich Minister of Education, all schools and universities were brought under its authority. What changed? For one thing, community service became compulsory and lasted one full year. New "Nazified" (politically correct) courses were instituted, especially in racial science, while academic science classes deteriorated rapidly. Great instructors like Franck and Einstein were retired or were fired. Historians agree that academic standards fell dramatically.

It appears that nationalizing American schools is right around the corner. Despite stacks of thick, revolutionary bills, this school takeover is making very little noise.

The Hushed Takeover of American Education

Columnist Robert Holland calls it "The Hushed Takeover of American Education." His October 1993 *Washington Times* article links GOALS 2000 (Educate America Act) directly to OBE. "Although the term [OBE] isn't used, Outcome-Based Education plainly is the philosophy behind Clinton's [GOALS 2000] plan,"[11] says this article. Philosophically, both OBE and GOALS 2000 intend to tailor schools to the needs of industry, not education.

According to Holland, GOALS 2000 was heavily influenced by the "pro-OBE National Center on Education and the Economy's publication *America's Choice: High Skills or Low Wages.*" The article adds that GOALS 2000 "incorporates practically all of the Magaziner Commission's recommendations."[12] (For details, see chapter 4.) Therefore, it aligns itself with Labor's *SCANS*.

Is outcome-based education the arrow and GOALS 2000 the bow that will shoot OBE-type restructuring into schools throughout the nation?

Outcome-based education is ideal for helping students meet the national "volunteer" standards (outcomes). In the 28 March 1994 issue of *USA Today*, D. L. Cuddy, a former official of the U.S. Department of Education, agreed. He pointed out that one of Goals 2000's new councils will certify " 'what all students should *know* and be able to *do*'— the widely objectionable 'outcome-based education.' "[13] States legislating outcome-based education use those identical words (*know* and be able to *do*). Will Clinton's education bills automatically give grant money to states only if they will use some form of the controversial OBE? Although it doesn't mandate outcome-based education, its vague language "seems to mandate OBE strategy," says a concerned former Indiana state senator.[14]

Cuddy says that GOALS 2000 companion bill HR6 "specifically mentions 'outcome performance indicators,' as well as other language associated with OBE, such as students allowed 'to progress at their own pace' (most students procrastinate), and 'cooperative learning' (with group grades and most of the workload usually placed upon brighter students)."[15]

"The Hushed Takeover of American Education" sums up GOALS 2000 by saying that law would put machinery in place for a national school board, a national curriculum, and national performance standards "specifying the skills and attitudes students need to be productive cogs in the New World Order."[16]

More Than an Oil Change—It's an Entire System

Strong language. But, what's happening in our country is unprecedented. The bill itself says the government wants to "revitalize" schools by "fundamentally changing the *entire system of public education*" (emphasis added).[17] Why change the *entire* system unless you intend to change the historic mission of schools? Does this mean school's primary purpose will be to produce workers, not thinkers? Will students start apprenticeships at age sixteen? Will federal engineers determine who will be needed in their planned work force of tomorrow? Will a Certificate of Initial Mastery be required?

To receive federal GOALS 2000 dollars, will states push through legislation mandating that high schools use the Certificate of Initial Mastery "diploma"? "Although the bill [GOALS 2000] does not specifically call for the adoption of a Certificate of Initial Mastery [CIM]," says a National Centers publication, "it does lay the foundation that a certificate could build upon."[18] This CIM plan has been driven smoothly—but ever so quietly—by social planners. GOALS 2000's National Education Goals Panel has begun to advocate the development of an *examination system consistent* with the creation of a *Certificate of Initial Mastery,*" wrote Ira Magaziner and Hillary Rodham Clinton in 1992 (emphasis added).[19]

GOALS 2000 or Goals 1984

George Orwell's futuristic novel *1984* projected a similar exam and tracking system. The book describes an elite Inner Party existing below Big Brother. The Outer Party consisted of dumb masses, numbering 85 percent of the population. "Admission to either branch of the Party is by examination, taken at the age of sixteen."[20]

In Orwell's *1984*, the mass of semiliterate workers fueled the economy while social planners decided policy. Each was tracked into his or her station at age sixteen. Dangers abound when education marches to the orders of the elite in business, government, and labor.

If federal laws will fundamentally change the "entire system of public education," are there some unseen players standing in the wings? Maybe labor, nonprofit foundations, and big business each have a scheme of how to totally redo American education. After all, they view your children as their human resources.

Eviscerating Local School Boards

Most Americans would never want to spell school S-T-A-T-E. Especially if they realize that nationalizing education will mean that local *elected* school boards essentially would be eviscerated. This education takeover creates an *unelected* federal school board.

At the heart of GOALS 2000 is a powerful, unelected new agency called the National Education Standards and Improvement Council. The *New York Times* says it "would function like a national school board."[21] Similar to the local school board—except on a national level—these powerful council members will certify curriculum standards (national) and tests (state). That's alarming. It's especially frightening because all twenty members are appointed by the president, and there's no requirement for bipartisanship.

It is frightening; however, not surprising. In chapter 2 we mentioned that local school boards were thought of as "Philistines" to be conquered. Then, Moses-like OBE/restructuring agents could enter the Promised Land.[22] Chester Finn, who was a chief architect of President Bush's America 2000, agrees. Finn believes local school boards are "preservers" of "encrusted practices." He says now "we need change agents in charge"[23] to bring in radical reform.

Finn ridicules "local control" and favors "change agents"[24] who will aggressively drive reform. Does he really want to eliminate local school boards? After all, citizens pay taxes. They deserve to elect someone who will represent their views. If a school board adopts OBE, and, if parents find their children aren't learning, they can always elect a new board. Under a federal school board, citizens would have no such recourse.

In the article "Reinventing 'Local Control of Education,'" Finn tells the reader, "Breathe deeply. What if we were to declare local boards . . . archaic?" Before that reader has time to exhale, Finn adds that local boards "are not just superfluous. They are also dysfunctional."[25]

An abundance of school board seats were filled by "dysfunctional" citizens opposing OBE in reaction to Pennsylvania bureaucrats' forcing through statewide performance-based education (OBE). After the election, a bill suddenly appeared in the legislature to put state officials in charge of training classes for local school boards. If members failed the course, they could be ousted.[26]

Sean Duffy, president of the Pennsylvania Leadership Council said, "It's aimed at the Religious Right. This is a way to dampen dissent and enthusiasm for change [end OBE]. They will hold people hostage and give them propaganda."[27] Public outcry defeated the bill, but the press secretary from the Department of Education said they will keep pushing for mandatory training.[28]

Ernest Boyer, president of the Carnegie Foundation (who, as we mentioned earlier, cheered when Pennsylvania eliminated the Carnegie Unit requirement), said, "I think for the first time America is more preoccupied with national results than local school control."[29]

Says who? Not parents. They stand tall and say, "School reform promoting taxation without representation—either on the local level, or in GOALS 2000—is not only dysfunctional; it is tyranny."

How Do You Spell Outcome-Based Education? G-O-A-L-S 2-0-0-0

During his fight to stop this bill, Texas Representative Dick Armey sent a letter to his peers in Congress entitled, "How Do You Spell Outcome-Based Education? G-O-A-L-S 2-0-0-0." He explained, "The Goals 2000 campaign is consciously patterned on states' OBE efforts."[30] Representative Armey was saying that OBE is this bill's delivery system in the local school.

Let's back up a moment; where did the national goals, such as citizenship, come from?

Governors' Goals

In stark contrast to Ronald Reagan, who wanted to abolish the Department of Education, George Bush dreamed of being remembered as "The Education President." To capture that dream, at the 1989 Education Summit at Charlottesville, Virginia, President Bush and governors from fifty states agreed to establish National Education Goals.

Several months later, reform was again launched in Wichita, Kansas, at the 1989 Governors Conference on Education. To the uninitiated, this was a strange coming-out party for education reform. Most speakers' remarks dealt more with a liberal social agenda than reform strategies to improve reading or math.

Rather than "re-form," speakers spoke in terms of "re-make." Lamar Alexander, the governor from Tennessee, said, "It's better to start from scratch to create one new American school." He stressed that the "school might need to serve the pregnant mother."[31]

Shirley McCune, senior director of the Mid-Continent Regional Educational Laboratory, said, "We no longer see the teaching of facts and information as the primary outcome of education."[32] In the audience, a few people looked uneasy, but the majority of listeners smiled appreciatively. Her talk was sprinkled with radical phrases, such as "total transformation" and "total restructuring." She explained, "You can't go into rural areas. You can't go into the churches, you can't go into government or into business, and hide from that fact that what we are facing is a total restructuring of the society."[33]

When change agents like McCune talk about "total restructuring," they mean *total*. They see their role as social engineers. Schools must be re-made to begin teaching at age zero and continue throughout a citizen's entire life. The government should set standards and content. Then, it must monitor citizens to ensure that state-defined outcomes are mastered.

In 1990, six voluntary national goals were unveiled.

America 2000 = GOALS 2000

Bush tied these goals into an attractive legislative package and covered it with America 2000 wrapping paper. But, Congress didn't buy it.

Because restructuring is a bipartisan effort, when Bill Clinton became president, he grabbed the six prepackaged goals, then rewrapped them with GOALS 2000 paper. Same goals, different political party. Ironically, although President Bush dreamed of becoming "The Education President," history will, no doubt, remember the man who defeated him by assigning President Clinton that epitaph.

Presto, New Goals

When President Clinton took the America 2000/ GOALS 2000 package from Bush, the goals were *voluntary*. National voluntary goals seemed like a reasonable idea. But, President Clinton made the goals *law*. There had been *six* goals, but President Clinton added two more, bringing the total to *eight*.

Did you hear anyone ask for two more laws/goals? A short time before GOALS 2000 was voted on, they were written into the bill. They just appeared during the legislative process. Both are targeted at adults, not children. They are goal number four for teachers, and goal number eight to strengthen partnerships. They mandate that every school promote partnerships that will increase parental involvement. Will the number of goals continue to increase?

Looking at America's reform from a global perspective may help answer that question. In 1990, the United Nations/World Bank sponsored World Conference on Education for All, which met in Thailand. That international education conference hammered out goals ("articles") similar to the six goals President Bush announced that same year.

The World Conference, however, produced not six goals, but ten—number seven, for example, is "Strengthening Partnerships."[34] If we add more goals, will they be similar to those endorsed by the World Conference? Their number nine goal is "Mobilizing Resources" ("It will be essential to mobilize existing and new financial and human resources, public, private and voluntary.").[35] And, goal number ten is "Strengthening International Solidarity" ("It requires international solidarity . . . in order to redress existing economic disparities").[36]

Eight National Goals

Let's look at America's eight national goals:[37]

1. *School Readiness:* By the year 2000, all children in America will start school ready to learn.

2. *School Completion:* By the year 2000, the high school graduation rate will increase to at least 90 percent.

3. *Student Achievement and Citizenship:* By the year 2000, all students will leave grades 4, 8, and 12 having demonstrated competency over challenging subject matter including English, mathematics, science, foreign languages, civics and government, economics, arts, history, and geography.

4. *Teacher Education and Professional Development:* By the year 2000, the nation's teaching force will have access to programs for the continued improvement of their professional skills.

5. *Mathematics and Science:* By the year 2000, the United States students will be first in the world in mathematics and science achievement.

6. *Adult Literacy and Lifelong Learning:* By the year 2000, every adult American will be literate and will possess the knowledge and skills necessary to compete in a global economy and exercise the rights and responsibilities of citizenship.

7. *Safe, Disciplined, and Alcohol-and Drug-Free Schools:* By the year 2000, every school in the United states will be free of drugs, violence, and the unauthorized presence of firearms and alcohol and will offer a disciplined environment conducive to learning.

8. *Parental Participation:* By the year 2000, every school will promote partnerships that will increase parental involvement and participation in promoting the social, emotional, and academic growth of children.

Actually, those goals sound pretty good. Most people would be comfortable adding them to a family's holiday wish list. But, because the mold of traditional school is being destroyed, things are no longer as they seem. Our educational system is being totally restructured to meet these national goals or outcomes.

Attitudes and values must conform to the current politically correct standards. Will human capital be educated, then directed into occupations according to society's needs? If so, this will require a government-supervised cradle-to-grave education.

Uncle Sam's responsibility for us will not end at the legal dropout age or graduation. For decades, compulsory school attendance has been enforced by law. After high school, the government laws concerning education ended. Under GOALS 2000, will adults be educated in how to be parents and how to get recertified for new jobs? That's lifelong learning. You might read the eight goals again. See it now? The governor of Utah sees it, and he likes the idea:

"The goals [national goals] are 'cradle to grave' and cover the preschool years and the after school years,"[38] writes Utah's Governor Leavitt, in a letter encouraging his state to continue its alignment with these national education goals. Because OBE is the transmission belt to drive federal education restructuring at the local level, Utah is ready and waiting. According to a 1991 study funded by Utah's Office of Education, "Utah is unique in the extent to which OBE has been implemented, with all districts using OBE to some degree."[39]

Again, let's look at the goals.

Holding Goals under a Magnifying Glass

Now, let's open up the actual GOALS 2000 bill and look closely at the first three goals. In the law, beneath each goal is listed specific objectives (outcomes). They mandate how to meet that goal.

Goal Number One: School Readiness

1. "All children in America will start school ready to

learn."[40] Ready to learn what? This goal doesn't say ready to read or do math. Might teaching Judeo/Christian beliefs thwart a child's readiness to learn "cultural diversity"—if "diversity" includes pedophiles? (Teaching cultural diversity is mandated in goal number three.[41])

2. "Every parent . . . will . . . devote time each day to helping . . . preschool child learn."[42] Who will monitor whether a parent spends time *each* day? Will self-reports be required? Will a parent educator come into your home to check compliance? (This bill also establishes an early intervention program—birth through age five.[43] This program provides for "regular visits with families by certified parents as teachers."[44])

3. "Children will receive . . . health care needed." Will the school supervise prenatal and postnatal care? Should health care be part of a school's mission? (Remember, at the Kansas Governors Conference, Lamar Alexander said schools might be serving pregnant mothers. This legislation calls for redesigning schools to become social services centers for children and adults, providers of what the bill calls "one-stop shopping."[45]) Most schools have only collected information about kindergarten immunizations; will federal data collection on children increase? The *Wall Street Journal* projects that the National Goals Panel will recommend "schools start collecting reams of new information on individual students" (from birthweight to dentist appointments to voter registration).[46] How will this long-term collection of data be kept private?

Goal Number Two: School Completion

1. "The Nation must dramatically reduce its school dropout rate." Will schools stop using competitive grades so students will no longer fail? *US News & World Report* says GOALS 2000 will help by "lowering the education bar."[47] Highlighted in America 2000/GOALS 2000 literature, a middle school graded students *P* (Proficient) and *I* (In Progress). Subject areas were "Sense of Self," "Appreciation of Change," and "Perspective Consciousness."[48] OBE's

theme, "all shall succeed," will prevent failure, and thus improve graduation statistics.

Goal Number Three:
Student Achievement and Citizenship

1. "Students will leave grades 4, 8, and 12 having demonstrated competency." Will competency be measured by a "voluntary" national assessment test? National outcome-based education (OBE)? National curriculum?

2. "All students will be involved in . . . community service." Is *mandated* volunteerism unconstitutional? Yes. And, David Moralis, who was denied his diploma, can tell you this goal is not academic.

3. "All students will be knowledgeable about diverse cultural heritage." Will this mandate multicultural studies (which often deprecate European/Western tradition and glorify underdeveloped cultures)? Might special interest groups such as transvestites, in the name of cultural diversity, demand that health class include the study of *all* sexual preferences and practices?

Goal Number Five: Mathematics and Science

1. "The number of United States undergraduate and graduate students, especially women and minorities, who complete degrees in mathematics, science, and engineering will increase significantly." Might this discriminate against non-minority males? How would meeting this goal affect a non-minority student during a college admission process?

The 1993 preliminary draft of the national standards for math, *Assessment Standards For School Mathematics*, sounds more like a political essay than a manual on logic and numbers. "Equity is one of the highest and noblest priorities in our schools."[49] It continues to explain that "our . . . view of equity has changed," so now each student should have access to math that includes "high-order thinking." Does that mean math problems will now be loaded with "gender-correct" word problems? It goes on to say that the "eurocentric, middle class, predominantly male perspective" will change.[50] With this approach, what kind of math assessments will your child have to pass?

Goal Number Seven: Safe, Disciplined, and Alcohol-and-Drug-Free Schools

1. "Every school should work to eliminate sexual harassment." How do you determine if children are harassing the opposite sex or simply being playful? Should government schools be measuring nonsexist values? Second graders at Jensen Elementary School in Iowa were given the same survey in the fall (pretest) and again in the spring (post-test). Questions were, "Are most girls better at math than boys?" "Do just girls take piano lessons?" "Are the best doctors usually men?"[51]

Grassley Amendment: Pupil Rights

Intrusive school surveys and bizarre tests, sent by parents of children in OBE schools, flooded the office of U. S. Sen. Charles E. Grassley (Iowa). He was convinced. Somehow he had to protect children from the psychologically damaging potential of OBE's national counterpart—GOALS 2000.

Together with a few parents who were experts in OBE, Senator Grassley forged a Protection of Pupil Rights amendment to GOALS 2000. Grassley's 1994 amendment may be the finest pupil rights protection the nation has ever had. Possibly his colleagues also saw the need for such protection as part of GOAL 2000 because the bill was passed by a huge margin.

Children can now opt out of any survey, test, or evaluation that reveals political affiliations, sexual behavior, income, psychological problems—or anything potentially embarrassing. Unfortunately, it only protects students from intrusive *federally* funded material.

Also known as the Protection of Pupil Rights, it should be available to all parents in their local school districts. Anti-OBE groups now use Grassley's amendment as a prototype for state legislation. That's the one bright spot in a bill many fear will federalize America's schools.

GOALS 2000's Lighthouse

"Goals 2000 takes OBE national."[52] That's what Rep. Dick Armey tried to tell his fellow legislators in the House, but the bill was thick with pages. Capitol Hill was buzzing with health care plans, and the list of eight national goals looked just fine, so it passed.

How will GOALS 2000 affect states? Does it take outcome-based education national? "Goals 2000 is, in a way, a national version of KERA (Kentucky Education Reform Act)," said U.S. Education Secretary Richard Riley.

Although Kentucky is in its fourth year of reform, two-thirds of its schools, based on state tests, are "in decline."[53] Not very impressive. Carnegie Corporation hired an ex-FBI agent as a "watchdog" to make sure school boards and state officials carry out the sweeping reform.[54] Not very spontaneous. The new assessment testing alone cost $80 million for five years, $50 million more than was estimated.[55] Not very inexpensive. And, in 1994, angry citizens stormed the capitol carrying "EEF U KEN REED THES THANK KERA" posters. Not very funny.

Like GOALS 2000, which passed with yet-unseen standards, Kentucky's education act was approved without outcomes. Now, Kentucky has seventy-five outcomes. Schools, with their social service resource centers, provide one-stop shopping. Most schools use some model of OBE, and preschool education is being pushed into schools.

Angie, vice president of the Parent Teacher Organization (PTO) in an OBE school, cries out in frustration saying, "multi-age classrooms, no grades in elementary school (might make some kids feel bad), de-emphasizing spelling and basic math, and 'integrating' all subjects. What this means is there are fewer subjects for academically interested children."

Just as upsetting as the lackluster academics is the escalation of social services within the school. Angie says that "family resource centers in the schools take up classroom space and cost a lot. In our school they run programs on childbirth and day care, which have nothing to do with education."

She continues,

> The federal government announced a couple weeks before school opened that a new preschool had to be opened in our elementary school—so a classroom was vacated, and the preschoolers marched in. Only problem—not enough needy people qualified since we have other such preschools in the other county schools. So . . . there was a big push to identify all possible kids in the community who might possibly need this service. I thought one purpose of government was to teach people how to get off government assistance instead of begging more people to get it.[56]

President Clinton's GOALS 2000: Educate America Act would help states "duplicate what Kentucky has done and is doing," points out U.S. Secretary of Education Riley.[57]

GOALS 2000: Golden Calf

The Elementary and Secondary Education Act (ESEA or HR 6) is GOALS 2000's cash register. GOALS 2000's price tag is $400 million,[58] and its companion, HR 6, is a pricey $9.5 billion.[59] It's your taxpayer money that the federal government is willing to share with the states—if they do the new reform.

Top-Down Control

"If I had ever whispered 'national standards,' I think I would have lost my job," said Ernest Boyer. "We bent over backwards fifteen years ago so that no one would think we were interfering."[60] Many Americans do think government is interfering.

It is top-down management. Government schools, using OBE-ish education, are interested in molding children's minds, even if it's in the high-sounding name of "equity."

Where freedom of the mind is concerned, the Bill of Rights was adopted to limit government coercion by putting expression, belief, and privacy out of reach of political majorities. Stephen Aaron, professor of legal studies at the University of Massachusetts, looks at this federal education bill and says, "An education bill of rights is essential . . . [to protect us] from change so fundamental that it amounts to a reconstitution of education."[61]

Grassroots America is responding. In 1994, Colorado passed a Tenth Amendment Resolution. It says that the role of the state in providing for the education of its people is reserved to the parents, the state, and the local school district.[62] Other states are following Colorado's lead.

Hushing the Truth to Push an Agenda

Does the federal government have to dive into the states to rescue education? Do we really need to break the mold of traditional education? Is education in America really making it a "nation at risk"?

Not according to the Sandia National Laboratories. In 1990, they were charged by the government to study our K–12 public schools. Everyone knew America's education was in "crisis," and Sandia's study would prove it. Instead, they revealed "much of the current rhetoric goes well beyond assisting reform and actually hinders it." The Sandia National Laboratories official findings contradicted President Bush's national agenda for reform. Our schools were performing quite well.

But, according to Daniel Tanner's article in the *Phi Delta Kappan*, "The Sandia Report was subjected to repeated refereeing, which effectively prevented the study from being published in a timely fashion."[63] Tanner believes the study was hushed.

Does This National Reform Include Parents?

"We all have to work together—business and government, labor and educators—to make things happen,"[64] says

President Clinton. Notice, in that statement, "we" includes business, government, labor, and educators. What stakeholder is missing? Will restructuring's Brave New "Family" include parents?

Endnotes

1. Public Law 103-227, Title I. Sec. 201. (3)(B)(iii).

2. According to the Office of Legislative Information, 1,646 bills dealt with education, school, and teaching.

3. Public Law 103-227, Part D. Sec. 1052. (4)(D).

4. The Tenth Amendment: "The powers not delegated to the United States by the Constitution, nor prohibited by it to the states, are reserved to the states respectively, or to the people."

5. William Celis III, "New Education Legislation Defines Federal Role in Nation's Classrooms," *New York Times*, 30 March 1994, B10.

6. Ibid.

7. Diane Ravitch, "Clinton's Math: More Gets Less," *New York Times*, 26 May 1993, A21.

8. Senator Judd Gregg, "A Federal Grab For Control Of Schools," *Washington Times*, 31 January 1994.

9. Daniel Tanner, "A Nation 'Truly' At Risk," *Phi Delta Kappan* (December 1993): 292, 293.

10. Ibid., and "Perspectives On Education In America: An Annotated Briefing," *Journal of Educational Research* (June 1993): 261–310.

11. Robert Holland, "The Hushed Takeover Of American Education," *Washington Times*, 15 November 1993, A19.

12. Ibid.

13. D.L. Cuddy, "Beware This Power Grab," *USA Today*, 28 March 1994, 12A.

14. Joan M. Gubbins, "GOALS 2000: Educate America Act," *Our Kids Report Card* (June/July): 4.

15. D. L. Cuddy, "Will Senate Approve School Takeover?" *Richmond Times-Dispatch*, 25 May 1994, A17.

16. Holland, "The Hushed Takeover."

17. GOALS 2000: Educate America Act, 21 March 1994, Sec. 301 (5), 35.

18. "States Begin Developing the Certificate Of Initial Mastery" (Washington DC: National Center On Education And The Economy, 1994), 2.

19. Hillary Rodham Clinton and Ira Magaziner, "Will America Choose High Skills Or Low Wages?" *Educational Leadership* (March 1992): 13.

20. George Orwell, *1984* (New York: New American Library, 1949), 172.

21. Ravitch, "Clinton's Math: More Gets Less," A21.

22. Alan November, "The Promised Land," *Electronic Learning* (September 1992): 20.

23. Chester E. Finn, Jr., "Reinventing Local Control," *Education Week* (23 January 1991): 40, 32.

24. Ibid., 32.

25. Ibid.

26. Carol Innerst, "Plan To Train School Boards Bashed As Pa. 'Brainwash,'" *Washington Times*, 15 February 1994, A4.

27. Ibid.

28. Ibid.

29. Finn, Jr., "Reinventing Local Control," 32.

30. Letter by U. S. Rep. Dick Armey, 6 October 1993.

31. Video of Governors Conference, Kansas, 2 November 1989.

32. Ibid.

33. Ibid.

34. *Final Report: World Conference On Education For All: Meeting Basic Learning Needs* (New York: Inter-Agency Commission, WCEFA, UNDP, UNESCO, UNICEF, World Bank, March 1990), 47.

35. Ibid., 48.

36. Ibid.

37. GOALS 2000: Educate America Act, Title I, Sec. 102, 7–9.

38. Letter from Utah Gov. Michael O. Leavitt and State Superintendent of Public Instruction Scott W. Bean, 30 September 1993.

39. Research and Development Consultants, *OBE In Utah: A Study of Outcome Based Education In Utah Executive Summary* (1991), 10.

40. GOALS 2000: Educate America Act, Title I, Sec. 102, (1)(B)(i), 7.

41. Ibid., Sec. 102, (3)(B)(vi), 8.

42. Ibid., Sec. 102, (1)(B)(ii), 7.

43. Ibid., Sec. 405, (1)(A), 68.

44. Ibid., Sec. 405, (1)(C)(i), 68.

45. Ibid., Sec. 306, (D)(f)(2), 42.

46. Rochelle Sharpe, "Panel To Suggest U.S. Schools Collect More Comprehensive Data On Students," *Wall Street Journal*, 21 April 1993, A4.

47. John Leo, "Lowering The Education Bar," *US News & World Report* (21 June 1993): 19.

48. *AMERICA 2000 Community Update*, U.S. Department of Education (30 October 1992).

49. *Assessment Standards For School Mathematics, Working Draft* (National Council of Teachers of Mathematics, October 1993), 27.

50. Ibid., 12.

51. Student survey, Jensen Elementary School, October 1992.

52. Letter by U. S. Rep. Dick Armey, 6 October 1993.

53. Lucy May, "Two-Thirds Of Schools Mediocre At Best, Boysen Says," *Lexington Herald-Leader*, 18 February 1994, 1A.

54. The Associated Press, "School Reform Monitors Funded, Carnegie Grant Helps Group Ensure Changes Are Made," *Cincinnati Inquirer*, 22 January 1991.

55. Eric Gregory, "Boysen Seeks $80 Million To Test Students," *Lexington Herald-Leader*, 30 July 91, A4.

56. Letter from Angie (last name withheld), 12 February 1994.

57. Lucy May, "U.S. Education Chief Lauds Kentucky Reform" *Lexington Herald Leader*, 16 October 1993, C3.

58. Michel Barone, "Setting School Standards—Quietly," *US News & World Report* (14 February 1994): 28.

59. "GOALS 2000 Committee Report," U.S. senate, 13 July 1993, 7.

60. Celis, "New Education Legislation."

61. Stephen Aron, "Nationalize Education and Take Away Choice?" *Hartford Courant*, 13 February 1994.

62. State of Colorado Senate Joint Resolution 94–13, 1 March 1994.

63. Tanner, "A Nation 'Truly' At Risk," 291.

64. "GOALS 2000," *Community Update*, U.S. Department of Education (May 1993).

SIX

BRAVE NEW FAMILY

We have cut the links between child and parent. Children will be taken from their mothers at birth, as one takes eggs from a hen.

—George Orwell, *1984*

Frightened and confused, the four young sisters held hands while the Department of Human Services officials herded them from their elementary school. The girls were ages six to eleven.

An emergency order charged their parents with abuse and neglect. Nancy, a welfare supervisor, stated the parents were also overprotective, refusing to allow their youngsters on school field trips. Another welfare investigator emphasized the children were placed in protective foster care mainly because of neglected teeth.

Earlier, their father tried to explain that his children were being seen by a dentist, but the social worker had hung up the phone, not letting him finish. Bewildered, the father, Raymond McIntosh, told reporters, "They took my children because of cavities."[1]

Social workers testified they were unaware the McIntoshes had taken their girls to the dentist. However, other concerns justified custody—extreme parental overprotection, no school field trips.

Mr. McIntosh said he only withheld permission for one trip, a swimming program. He feared his children might catch a cold. After explaining the overprotectiveness and producing evidence that the girls were seeing a dentist, his daughters were returned home.[2] But, charges of abuse will remain on the McIntosh record permanently.

In America?

Unbelievable. State officials don't interfere like that, not in America. But, it is true, every detail. And, it's becoming increasingly common.

Someone who doesn't approve of spanking (physical abuse) or of teaching children about hell (emotional abuse) can anonymously call a social worker to report any parent. Although 60 percent of reported abuse cases are unsubstantiated, children may be removed from home for *suspected* neglect or abuse.[3]

Teachers in most states are required to report suspected abuse. Failure to report can generate up to a year in prison with a hefty fine.[4]

Even before a child starts school, an adult's fitness as a parent will be evaluated. Programs closely aligned with OBE's philosophy will send "home educators" into your house, even into your maternity ward.

OBE's brave new "family" will be school. Today, the government school is fast becoming the center of every American community. Soon, this government building will be the vortex of your child's world.

In Your Home?

You've just arrived home with your newborn baby. When your district high school sends a "parent educator" to your house, you welcome her. Since schools became a center for health and social services, all parents are assigned a parent educator.

With clipboard tucked under one arm, the kind-looking woman explains your sweet baby is entitled to every state service. "To prevent an 'at risk' situation, I'll help you become the child's first teacher," she says. You notice she doesn't say the word *mother*, and ask her why.

"Some families have two daddies and no mother. No matter what situation or sexual preference, we want all caregivers treated equally."

Her eyes scan the room as she talks. She notices as you lift an eyebrow questioningly. "Part of my job is checking homes for environmental suitability," she says and smiles, until she spots the Bible on the endtable. "We're here to help you understand your child is unique. He must be allowed to develop his own beliefs, his own values."

Unfortunately your voice rises an octave as you defend yourself. "I won't force him to believe as I do. But, I have the right to bring him up in my religion."

"I'm religious myself," she says. "But, we find it's best when children have a number of choices." Then she asks, "Do you easily become irritated?" The parent educator checks something on her clipboard.

She admires the pink and blue baby quilt you made. While handing you a pamphlet with helpful hints about childproofing the house, she asks rhetorically, "Wouldn't it be wonderful if we could child-proof homes against abuse, like spanking?" She adds, "We offer counseling in discipline, family planning, everything."

As she leaves, the parent educator says, "See you in about six weeks. Together we'll make sure baby 'starts school ready to learn.'[5] After all, that first National Goal is law now, you know." She gets in an automobile and drives off to submit her report to the local school.

Unlike Mr. and Mrs. McIntosh's experience, the second scenario is hypothetical. But, today every detail is in place to make it a reality. As illustrated in the story, restructuring puts social services, including parent educator programs, in schools. For instance, forty-four states now use the Parents As Teachers (PAT) program, with its parent educators. (Ironically, parent educators have to be neither parents nor teachers. They qualify through a five-day training session[6]).

Pregnant women are often recruited. An official from PAT National Center was quoted in a 1990 newspaper as saying, "Some of our parent educators follow expectant women around the supermarket so they can ask them whether they know about the program."[7]

Children and parents are evaluated. Evaluations are recorded, coded, and computerized. All twelve computer codes label the child "at risk." If the youngster doesn't fit into the first eleven "at risk" categories, the child automatically falls into the twelfth called "Other." There is no code for normal.[8]

Similar programs are called by different names. For example, according to a Carnegie task force report called *Starting Points*, Hawaii's Healthy Start Program provides an initial home visit for all families with newborns.[9]

"Whole Child" Express

How did America get to this point so quickly? It started with progressive education in the mid-sixties. That's when schools rerouted their direction. They jumped the railroad track from educating a youngster's intellect onto a new track of nurturing the whole child.

Progressive education stoked the engine by demanding that schools meet the whole child's needs—intellectual, social, physical, and emotional. Teaching self-esteem resulted in students introducing their conclusions in academic papers with "I feel" rather than "I think" or "I know." Academic studies began sharing precious class time with affective education (*Webster* says "affective" deals with emotions or feelings, not thought.)

In 1977, the *Washington Post* reported that progressive education's "new curriculum" was based on the work of the psychologist B.F. Skinner.[10] Skinner's Mastery Learning/OBE curriculum used his controversial behavioral modification, which trained students the same way he trained animals. Along with Skinner, OBE's "father," Benjamin Bloom, jumped aboard this "whole child" train with his belief that "the purpose of schools is to change thoughts, feelings, and actions of students."[11] Of course, Spady, Sizer, Goodlad, and others grabbed seats.

OBE's luggage included affective outcomes, school-based councils, early childhood education, one-track system, exit exams, peer tutoring, longer school days, year-round school, parent partnerships, multiage grouping, assessments, and much more.

When NEA officials and business elite brought Uncle Sam on board, his baggage looked just like OBE's, except it contained 1994s massive education laws like GOALS 2000. That would help pay OBE's ticket. A few parents caught glimpses of the train speeding by, but not one mom or dad was invited on board. Today, it's a runaway express.

Farewell Parents

OBE's Orwellian train is speeding away from school's original mission. Before the sixties, when schools still stressed the three Rs, America's public school system had produced the most literate nation in history. Beliefs, values, and physical wellness still belonged to families.

Historically, Americans have upheld the family's sacred right to control education. In fact, during the eighteenth century most everyone agreed with the philosopher John Locke who wrote,

> all parents, were by the law of nature "under an obligation to preserve, nourish, and educate the children" they had begotten; not as their own workmanship, but the workmanship of their own Maker.[12]

Parental authority over education was sovereignly ordained. It was etched in law. It was protected by courts. Therefore, it was respected by schools—until progressive education.

Welcome Partners

As parents relinquished more responsibility to the school, families' authority diminished. Now, government schools will take control. Through its partnership concept, schools first invite—then mandate—parents to become one of many partners in their own child's education.

Concerned parents asked, "Why should we become mere partners?" One father, a building contractor, compared this parent/school partnership to his contracting business. He explained he was owner of the houses he built; however, he always subcontracted companies, some to put in electricity, others to install carpet. They enhanced his homes. But, those electricians and carpet layers do not pretend to own the contractor's houses. Similarly, when he sends his children to school, he pays (subcontracts) for educational services. Period. He and his wife were sole owners of their children, not mere partners.

Other parents pointed out that human nature dictates that no two people can agree on every issue. Since schools are viewing so many families as dysfunctional, it was obvious to these skeptics the school would become senior partner—eventually casting all deciding votes. Would this government entity, called school, determine if children must attend a learning center, take Ritalin, be tracked into specific newly created Certificate of Advanced Mastery occupational careers?

But, since OBE propaganda framed opposition as "radical," these concerns were buried.

Although strongly encouraged by OBE literature, partnerships have been optional. Today, parent/school partnerships are law. GOALS 2000 legislates, "Every school will actively engage parents and families in a partnership."[13]

Why? Becoming partners mandates that families come on line supporting the school's radical shift from academic to career education. Using its assessments, outcomes, and social services, federal education will shape your child (its human capital). Dr. Shirley McCune, influential OBE advocate and director of the Mid-Continent Regional Educational Laboratory, tells us, "We no longer see the teaching of facts and information as the primary outcome of education."[14] Education is adopting a new mission. She says that schools are leaving "schooling business" to go into "human resource development."[15]

Children or Human Resources?

For the first time in American history, the individual child is no longer educated for the parents. Instead, the parents must educate their "human resource" for the school. Is this another education fad that will pass with time? Or a serious step toward socialism?

"What we're into is the total restructuring of society," Dr. McCune said in her address at the 1989 National Governor's Conference on Education. Another speaker, future U.S. Secretary of Education Lamar Alexander, called for new American schools that would "be open year round" and "serve children from three months to age eighteen."[16]

The Family Is Dead, Long Live the School

Schools taking babies from the nursery at age three months? Sounds like the first victim of this "total restructuring of society" will be the family. As OBE spreads, watch for:

- schools eliminating the traditional two parent family as the ideal
- schools undermining parental authority
- schools redefining family
- schools becoming one-stop shopping for a child's every need

When America's brave new family is unveiled, what will it be?

Family Disappearing Act

At an elementary school in Louisville, Kentucky, a traveling library committee busily sorted out books to be taken and sold. "How do you decide which books should be weeded out?" asked Sharon, a math tutor. The committee told her one criteria was the pictures. They explained to Sharon, "We don't want the student who doesn't live with two parents to feel bad when he or she reads. So we remove any books with pictures of the nuclear family, a mom, dad, and child."[17]

What unspoken message does that send to all elementary students? School books without pictures of a traditional family subliminally shout, "The nuclear family is dead!" to impressionable minds.

Some educators place books in schools to introduce "new" families. Oregon's *Register-Guard* reports that *Heather Has Two Mommies* and *Daddy's Roommate* (picture books depicting a lesbian and a homosexual live-in relationship) were recently supplied to about thirty preschool libraries in Lane County, Oregon. Angry parents voiced concern that their four- and five-year-olds would get the message "homosexuality is good" and the equal of marriage.[18]

In Cottage Grove, Oregon (where the nation's first Certificate of Initial Mastery was given), Head Start preschool teachers received a notice: classroom bulletin boards will "include lesbian/gay families in family units."[19] Why choose a controversial group which only represents *one percent* of American males?[20] What next? Will posters depict live-in relationships of transvestites, pedophiles, cannibals?

That might fit into Oklahoma's curriculum. Like every other state, Oklahoma's OBE embraces the affective domain to change feelings, attitudes, and values. One state outcome listed for first grade is, "The student will identify different types of family structures, so that no single type [traditional] is seen as the only possible one."[21]

Abusing the Traditional Family

While OBE marches under the banner of "new" families, the old family is taking a beating. To see what is happening to a parent's role, let's examine a test from the affluent Blue Valley District, Kansas. *First* graders must answer:

> Kaitlin is lying down watching television. Her dad comes in and lies down beside her. He puts his hands under her dress and begins to touch Kaitlin's vagina. Kaitlin's dad tells her to keep it a secret. Who could Kaitlin tell?[22]

The child's answers are scored and recorded. An attached paper states that this test is monitoring first graders' progress in meeting Kansas Outcome Eight: Students have the physical and emotional well-being necessary to live, learn, and work in a global society. Will this test help or hinder "emotional well-being"? Checking for signs of child abuse is laudable. But, will explicit scenarios plant unhealthy seeds of distrust in a child's mind? A book dealing with youngster's emotional needs, *Talking with Your Child about a Troubled World*, states that young children interpret situations literally, and they view issues on a personal level.[23] Next time daddy playfully tickles his first grader, will she dissolve into innocent giggles—or be suspicious of her own father?

Meanwhile, in another state, in an eleventh-grade home economics class, a handout said, "Rearrange the letters in the word PARENTS and you get the word ENTRAPS."[24]

Americans trust baseball and apple pie and schools. Kansas parents probably never suspected their first graders took that outcome test. And, mothers and fathers of students in the home economics class didn't realize that the teacher also told students, "The American family does not exist."[25]

Parents trust schools. But, do schools trust traditional families? After all, Norman Rockwell-type families still punish by spanking. They teach children moral absolutes. And, many ideas discussed around the kitchen table aren't politically correct. Will schools label these families intolerant, far Right, or dysfunctional?

OBE wants its system to include *all* children. Homeschoolers are now especially vulnerable. In some states, social workers harass homeschooling families. Expanding child abuse to include emotional as well as physical abuse sets a dangerous precedent. If social workers can cite homeschooling parents for child abuse, children can be funneled into the public school. For instance, in Iowa *truancy* was redefined to include lack of supervision as one definition of child abuse under that state's child welfare law. In 1989 and 1990, Iowans fought a legislative bill that would have classified the majority of homeschoolers as "truants."[26] The bill was defeated—by only one vote.

Redefining Family

OBE futurist Dr. Spady predicts the family will decline rapidly due to "increasing maternal employment and high divorce rates."[27] All OBE promoters agree. David Hornbeck prophesies, "It is clear that we are not going to return to . . . families in which one parent works and the other cares for the two children."[28]

If you remember, OBE demands that all outcomes (such as family life) revolve around future assumptions (predictions).[29] Crystal balls, however, are about as accurate as weather forecasts. Although OBE predicates the family will rapidly decline *due to more mothers working*, just the opposite is happening. "Reversing a decade-long trend, young women are opting out of the job market and staying home," announced *Barron's* in March 1994.[30] It's a new trend. This business journal stated "the traditional one-paycheck family (fathers breadwinner, mothers at home) is now the fastest growing household unit."[31]

Leaving briefcases and salary behind, mothers now prefer staying at home. Young mothers enthusiastically lead the exodus flocking from office to kitchen.[32] Contrary to OBE's prediction, this stay-at-home pendulum swing is to "keep the family whole."[33] Even promotional magazines for working females like *Working Woman* admits mothers are fleeing jobs to nurture families.[34]

Well, what about the predicated rising divorce rate? Again, not so. Broken homes have been on the downswing since 1991. Statistics from the National Center for Health show that, by 1991, divorce had dropped to its lowest point since the 1970s.[35]

Certainly the two-parent family is disappearing, isn't it? Not according to the U.S. Census Bureau—75 percent of children still live in two-parent homes.[36] And, young people are increasingly committed to marital permanence, says Dr. David Popenoe, sociologist at Rutgers University and co-chair of the Council on Families in America. He calls this 1990s profamily, cultural shift, "The New Familism."[37]

Susy (mentioned in our first chapter) read about a school in North Carolina which declared that the Norman Rockwell traditional family is dead.[38] Statistics disagree. The traditional family may have a bad cold, but is very much alive.

Yet, in an attempt to defend everyone's unique living situation, most OBE schools insist on defining family so broadly it creates nonfamily families. A typical definition from the nationally acclaimed OBE school in Farrell, Pennsylvania, is "FAMILY: Any person or persons who have a common bond of shared responsibility for each other and/ or a child or children in their care."[39]

Like so many "world-class" standards, a hoop is lowered so everyone can slam-dunk. Notice OBE's brave new family does not require blood, adoption, or any long-term commitment. In fact, this definition includes three gang members, two friends sharing an apartment, or twelve hundred students and their teachers (the school).

Is OBE redefining *family* to be *school* (a government building)? Newly mandated school advisory groups that are popping up around the county often are referred to as "family." In Milwaukee, an OBE school's staff, including social workers, whole language coordinators, advisors, house principal, and teachers—are called "extended family teachers." Students even receive an "extended family report card."[40]

A Department of Education's publication, *Ohio 2000 Discussion Guide*, calls multiage learning groups "family cohorts."[41] School calling itself "family" will cause a subtle but significant transfer in loyalty: from mom and dad to a government entity (school).

Community Hub: Government Building

Ohio's plan (based on outcomes and the national goals) calls for the school to become the hub of the community. This school will be open all twelve months, seven days a week (even the Sabbath), and include on-site social service agencies.[42] The "traditional school was part of the community." Now, "the community is part of the school."[43] It's happening throughout the nation. One school/center in Chelsea, Massachusetts, houses health clinics and a police substation.[44]

Laws should enforce schools to become the community center, according to the words of outcome-based enthusiast

David Hornbeck. He's past chairman of the board of the Carnegie Foundation for the Advancement of Teaching and was advisor to the Business Roundtable.

> At the state level, we should promulgate legislation that would create a new affirmative duty for government to assure the health and nonacademic well-being of each child until age eighteen. . . . That duty would begin during a mother's pregnancy with appropriate prenatal care, extend through the early years of life in the form of support of both mother and child, and as a child becomes school age, the duty would apply before and after school, on weekends and in the summer.[45]

Upon hearing about transforming schools into one-stop community centers, parents are beginning to say, "these changes remind us of 1940 Germany and the former U.S.S.R. Today we're no longer calling American schools, 'public schools.' We're reminding ourselves schools are 'government centers.' "

Cradle-to-Grave School

At the previously mentioned 1989 Governor's Education Conference, Lamar Alexander emphasized that new American schools would serve children from age three months to age eighteen. He added, "That may be a shocking thought to you."[46]

It's no surprise to an OBE school district in Farrell, Pennsylvania, which calls itself a "Cradle-to-Grave" school. The youngest students *are* three-and-a-half-months old. Farrell District, which is showered with grant and federal money, says their center is a "prescription for America."[47]

Actually, it looks utopian (or Orwellian). In one sprawling complex, the school houses teen parenting programs, day care, a high school, an elementary school, offices, plus a health clinic—where students and their families receive immunizations, dental exams, and pap smears. There's more. In the same building are mental health services, drug treatment offices, and a school-based case-worker. Service for *all* students (regardless of income) include free breakfast and lunch, year round.[48] Farrell's superintendent says, "We have to begin addressing the needs of students from birth."[49]

He adds, "Schools have to assume the responsibility of the once-solid American family."[50] (See page 121 for Farrell's definition of *family*.) "Book knowledge isn't enough," states the superintendent. Typical of OBE philosophy, career tests and social services must also meet the needs of the whole child—as well as the family.[51]

Questions arise. Can this tiny school district of about twelve hundred students depend on outside funds forever to meet its $8 million budget? Might the school (sometimes called center) become a "diaper ghetto" that warehouses children? Do schools want a multitude of unauthorized adults, some coming for drug treatment programs, accessing a building filled with young children? Will academics take a back seat to community social needs? Historically, American towns were built around a white steepled church. Should government schools, rather than houses of worship or privately run community centers, become a new hub? In other words, should a government building become a nucleus for cradle-to-grave care of citizens?

In an article called "Farrell Schools 'Womb to the Tomb,' " the superintendent says, "*every* school should develop family centers" (emphasis added).[52]

Kentucky's Statewide Centers

Cradle-to-grave care through government schools is the goal of America's runaway school restructuring train. It's what is wanted by business/government—not parents. Yet, throughout the nation, you can hear the sounds of bulldozers and hammers gutting old schools, rebuilding, or renovating. Parents aren't told, but it's in preparation for the OBE train with its preschool and social service cargo.

"School construction projects all over our state don't have anything to do with OBE-education reform, do they?" an OBE opponent from Washington State asked a friend from Kentucky. The Kentuckian laughed, "Sure does. Across my state we've emptied school buildings and expanded others for our Family Resource/Youth Service Centers."

We referred to Kentucky's KERA in other chapters. Because U.S. Secretary of Education Riley called Kentucky a "lighthouse" for the rest of the nation,[53] it's worth looking at that state again.

Kentucky's 1990 Education Reform Act (KERA) mandated that schools with children "at risk" include Family Resource/Youth Service Centers.[54] Quickly, more than two hundred centers appeared in or near schools. Much like Farrell's cradle-to-grave concept, KERA legislated that each center include:

- Full-time preschool child care starting at age two
- After school child care for four through twelve year olds
- Full-time child care during summers, holidays, and weekends
- Home visits for new mothers
- Social services including school based clinics, etc.[55]

Not surprisingly, within two short years, legislators expanded the law. Schools were mandated to provide centers—not just for those "at risk"—but for *all* children and their families.

A Disillusioned Parent

KERA decrees one (token) parent must sit on the centers' task force. After serving for more than two years, the first parent representative, Judy Paternostro, resigned, disgusted. In her resignation letter, Paternostro expresses deep concern over several issues. She says, "Parents are unaware that certain information gathered on their children or their family through the Centers is inaccessible to them."[56] Might the government use this information inappropriately? She asks, "Is the health and education bureaucracy of this state now responsible for every aspect of a family's well being?"[57]

Paternostro warns that centers take control "out of the hands of parents."[58] Minors can receive services without parental consent[59] for mental health counseling and school-based clinics' services.[60] Concern is well-grounded. For instance, in the area of mental health, the National Teachers Association's 1993 Resolutions call for every district to provide in-school counseling "for students who struggle with their sexual/gender orientation."[61] Wouldn't a parent want to know who is doing that mental health counseling?

And, although school-based clinics might start with honorable intentions, problems arise. In places like Baltimore, Maryland, for example, three years after school-based clinics were established, condom distribution began. Soon afterward, Norplant, a long-lasting birth control capsule implanted in a female's upper arm, was offered.[62]

Was the centers' task force aware that the Alan Guttmacher Institute (researcher for Planned Parenthood), which publishes *Family Planning Perspectives*, stated it couldn't find any evidence showing "school-based clinics reduce pregnancy"?[63]

"These Centers provide the perfect vehicle for the establishment of socialized medicine," adds Paternostro. (Incidentally, two major creators of *America's Choice*, which encourages youth centers, were the promotional team for national health, Ira Magaziner and Hillary Rodham Clinton.) Rather than strengthening families, she asks, "Won't encouraging dependency on government services through the schools have the opposite effect?"[64]

Centers: Express Delivery

With all these flashing yellow lights, what's the rush to turn schools into centers? Is it to force systemic change before citizens wake up? Thomas Boysen, Kentucky's commissioner of education explains that he promotes changing the whole system quickly because it's like riding a bicycle, rather than a tricycle. He says that if we go slowly "on the bike—on this systemic reform—we're going to lose our balance."[65] Does his analogy make sense? OBE/restructuring is about educating children, not riding bikes. Both OBE and centers are unproven, expensive, and controversial. Did Dr. Boysen ever hear of training wheels?

Following Kentucky's example, Alabama tried to rush reform laws through. A report from Business and Education Roundtable consultant David Hornbeck said that along with other elements of education based on outcomes (such as pre-kindergarten), centers in schools "should be a priority."[66] Kentucky State Rep. Thomas R. Kerr sent a letter to Alabama's legislators warning them to "steer clear of any proposal that uses components of outcome based education (OBE)."

In his letter, Representative Kerr said, "Let me warn you that KERA was rammed through in a very short span of time with no input from Kentucky educators and no time for public comment."[67] Alerted, parents and legislators in 1994 halted proposed legislation, temporarily.

All Schools Shall Be Family Centers

"By the year 2000, schools will become lifetime community learning centers," according to Iowa's K-12 Education Reform Study Committee.[68] Indiana, Kansas, Massachusetts, and many other states are humming the same tune. Although individual states may not realize it yet, centers are a federal concept.

The idea of nationwide school-based centers was sold to the government by the Labor's NEA,[69] the Business Roundtable, and tax-exempt foundations through organizations like the National Center. Today, a government public relations newsletter states that National GOALS 2000 Law "authorizes that by 1998, there will be at least one family resource center in every state."[70]

Again, why? Reinventing education ushers in a holistic approach to serving not only children, but entire families.[71] Sounding rather paternalistic, Oregon's Department of Education explains that "families must be supported so they can reach self-sufficiency."[72] This can only be done through the integration of social service with educational agencies, outcome-based promoters say. Oregon's task force says, "Schools are a source of stability and strength for students."[73] Do you get the idea the state (school) wants to fix your family?

What might these centers offer the American public beside social services? A hefty price tag. The National Centers' manual *America's Choice* says the youth center system will cost about \$8.2 billion per year.[74] *America's Choice* also proposes a frightening new law. It says, "once Youth Centers are established propose [that] child labor laws be amended." New laws would forbid people eighteen or under—without a Certificate of Initial Mastery—to get jobs.[75] Eventually, might age eighteen be extended to any adult without a CIM?

Can you hear that education train rushing into your hometown? Although the name will vary—Family and Children First, School-Based Youth Service Program, Youth/ Family Resource Centers, etc.—all schools are targeted to evolve into family resource centers. A national report by fifty teachers forecasted that "school buildings will be replaced by . . . 'community learning centers.' "[76]

U.S. Education and Human Services: Bedfellows

Parents aren't state approved, schools are. It's as simple as that. We mentioned that the U.S. Department of Education married the Labor Department to reinvent education. In 1993, the Department of Education also jumped in bed with the U.S. Department of Health and Human Services. They jointly produced the manual *Together We Can*. In it, Secretary of Education Richard Riley and Secretary of Health and Human Services Donna Shalala wrote that, through a "radical change," the government wants to "link education and human services."[77]

And, they mean radical. Have you heard about it? Press releases are as rare as Hawaiian snowstorms. The object is to centralize education, health clinics, every social service. Several Florida schools using the *Together We Can* model adopted the motto " 'one stop shopping' for social services and educational programs."[78]

Together We Can—Outcomes For Families

Transforming schools into one-stop shopping centers requires radical change, including increased control over families. *Together We Can* says the new system must be "outcomes oriented." Families will have outcomes.[79] Similar to the original six national goals for children, Ohio's Family and Children First law—modeled after *Together We Can*—lists six goals (outcomes) for the family. For example, goal number two states, "Families will understand and address the developmental needs of their children."[80]

Similar to OBE in schools, Ohio's communities will develop "measurable outcome indicators" telling families how to meet their outcomes.[81]

One "indicator" to meet family goal number two says that more young Ohio children *will* have access to preschool.[82] An education publication explains that "early childhood programs" shall be provided for "*all* three, four, and five-year-old economically disadvantaged children" (emphasis added). Funding will be available for *every* child whose family income is 185 percent of the poverty level.[83] That includes a two-parent family with three children living on an income of $31,099 or less.[84] Many families live within this "disadvantaged" level because of choice. They forego a two-income lifestyle so one parent can stay home with their little ones. Some are "disadvantaged" because a single parent may sacrifice to be at home with preschoolers. What if they don't want to send their toddlers to a state preschool?

How does recruiting preschool children protect the integrity of the family? As one Family First council member cautions, "In the future, preschool for disadvantaged families could become mandatory."[85]

Collaborative Governing Families

Who will control the new school/community's one-stop shopping? *Together We Can* says a new governing entity called "collaborative" will. In Ohio, collaborative are referred to as "county councils." According to *Together We Can*, the collaborative's responsibilities include creating a system able to "identify and meet the needs of every child and every family,"[86] providing ongoing data on the families served, and pushing for more federal financial support.[87]

David Hornbeck envisions the local collaborative to be

patterned after school boards. Thus, they would enjoy the "authority to raise taxes, as most school boards do."[88]

Over eighteen states are considering using the federal model of *Together We Can*. The Family and Children First initiatives will legislate linking schools with human services, thus turning schools into community centers.

But, Will It Help?

School becoming *in loco parentis* (standing in the place of parent) is the brainchild of the NEA, big business, and the federal government—not grassroots America. Before pushing the concept on local school districts, why not learn from those who've tried this "nanny school" experiment?

Sweden's six decade experiment with the nanny-state has been "thrown on the scrapheap of history," according to the *Wall Street Journal*. That newspaper reports that Sweden's education minister Beatrice Ask cautions Americans to think carefully before viewing schools as a center for the delivery of social services. Today, as social services disappear, grades, which were abolished for students under the age of fifteen, are being reintroduced. She said Swedish schools diluted education by trying to do too much. They "neglected their basic function—educating children."[89]

Family Is Not Spelled S-c-h-o-o-l

Yet, America's Orwellian train heads further from school's original mission—education. It's racing towards taking children from their mothers at birth, as one takes eggs from a hen. Why?

One way advocates of OBE frequently answer, "Schools have to take over because families are doing a terrible job." How do you argue with that? Two ways. First, because of the "whole child" theory, education got itself into an academic mess. Schools should clean up their house before trying to move into your private home. Second, schools can't become families.

Of course, in the life of children, schools occupy a valid place—teaching academic skills. Education in the three Rs is what youngsters need, and teaching is what school can do well. But, when education leaves that track to become the family, every child loses. The child "at risk" loses twice. He didn't have an adequate family, now he has no real school either. The "normal" child also loses. He still has a family, but no education.

OBE promoters contend there are kids coming to school who haven't eaten breakfast. Increasingly, children come to them from dysfunctional, one-parent families. What they say is true.

But, during the depression, kids arrived at school without breakfast and without shoes, and they were from disrupted families. During World War II, because their fathers went to war, children lived in single-parent homes. Mom became Rosie the Riveter—creating a nation of latchkey kids. Most families would have qualified as dysfunctional.

Over those years, the school proudly maintained its mission to teach academics. Educators promised, "We'll give all youth, especially children living in poverty, the tools they need to escape—so kids can climb as high as their hearts are big. Our goal is to instill academic skills." America continued to be one of the greatest countries in the history of civilization.

But today, using OBE, all children will lose twice. Schools won't emphasize academics. And, no matter how many social services and how much home intervention, school cannot be a family. What is happening in America?

Brave New Family

Simply put, America's new centers (formerly called schools) will assume responsibility to assure that human resources—from birth to death—are not "at risk." The state's work force must be shaped from birth, and parents (the breeders and feeders) are assigned the role of mere "partners" in this brave new family.

History often repeats itself. Earlier this century, one socialist state received worldwide acclaim. Its charismatic leader was also well-known as a school reformer. Listen to his words:

When an opponent declares, "I will not come over to your side," I calmly say, "Your child belongs to us already. . . . What are you? You will pass on. Your descendants, however, now stand in the new camp. In a short time they will know nothing else but this new community."[90]

—Adolf Hitler (speech of November 1933)

Endnotes

1. "Girls' Dental Problems Cause Family Legal Woes," *Dayton Daily News*, 15 December 1991, A6.

2. Ibid.

3. Constance Stapleton, "Could the State Take Your Child?" *Woman's Day* (18 May 1993): 56.

4. Ibid.

5. GOALS 2000: Educate America Act, Title I, Sec. 102, (1), (A) "By the year 2000, all children in America will start school ready to learn." Passed into law 31 March 1994.

6. Phone interview by author, with administrator at National Parents as Teachers Center, Missouri, 26 July 1994.

7. *St. Louis Post-Dispatch* (1990), as quoted in a paper by Laura Rogers, "The Road to '1984' Is through the Schoolhouse Door," 4.

8. Recordkeeping forms, "Risk Factor Definitions" (Missouri Department of Elementary & Secondary Education, 1989), 507, 508.

9. "Starting Points: Meeting the Needs of Our Youngest Children," (Carnegie Corporation of New York, April 1994), 72.

10. Lawrence Feinberg, "Competency Tests Set in 26 Schools," *Washington Post*, 1 August 1977, A1.

11. Benjamin S. Bloom, *All Our Children Learning* (New York: McGraw-Hill Book Company, 1981), 180.

12. John Locke, *Second Treatise of Government* (New York: The Macmillan Company, 1956), 28, 29.

13. GOALS 2000: Educate America Act, Title I, Sec. 102, (8), (B), (iii).

14. Video taken at Governor's Conference, Kansas, 2 November 1989.

15. Terri Minteer, "For Schools of the Future: They'll Become Centers of Learning," *Buenerton Sun*, 14 October 1989.

16. Video, Governor's Conference, Kansas.

17. "True Stories of 'Reformed' Education in Kentucky" (Parents and Professionals Involved in Education, September 1993), 10, and phone interview with Sharon by author, 31 July 1994.

18. Paul Neville, "Parents Protest Preschool Books on Homosexuality," *The Register-Guard*, 3 March 1994, 1A, A4, and Paul Neville, "OCA Rips Head Start Curriculum," *The Register-Guard*, 5 March 1994, C1, C2.

19. From notice sent to site teachers, Winter 1994. Because parents protested loudly, homosexual books were not placed in Cottage Grove classrooms. However, the books remain in almost thirty other school libraries in Lane County, Oregon.

20. "About 1% of American Men Homosexual, Survey Claims," *New York Times*, 15 April 1993, A1.

21. "Learner Outcomes Oklahoma State Competencies Grades First," (Oklahoma State Department of Education, n. d.), 59, 60.

22. Outcome test for first grade, from Blue Valley District, Kansas, September 1992.

23. Lynne S. Dumas, *Talking with Your Child about a Troubled World* (Columbine, New York: Fawcett, 1992), 58, 63.

24. Handout in an eleventh grade class in Pennsylvania, 2 November 1992.

25. Student notes from an eleventh grade home economics class in Pennsylvania.

26. "State House Briefing," *Des Moines Register*, 12 January 89, A2.

27. William G. Spady, "Future Trends, Considerations in Developing Exit Outcomes," *High Success Program on OBE* (September 1987), 3.

28. David W. Hornbeck and Lester M. Salamon, *Human Capital and America's Future* (Baltimore: Johns Hopkins University Press, 1991), 381.

29. Ron Brandt, "On Outcome-Based Education A Conversation with Bill Spady," *Educational Leadership* (December/January 1993): 68.

30. Maggie Mahar, "A Change of Place," *Barron's* (21 March 1994): 33.

31. Ibid.

32. Ibid., 35.

33. Ibid., 36.

34. Pamela Kruger, "Superwoman's Daughters: They Don't Want Your Job. They Don't Want Your Life. All Twenty something Women Want is to Change the Way America Works," *Working Woman* (May 1994): 60–62, 96, 98.

35. William J. Bennett, *The Index of Leading Cultural Indicators* (The Heritage Foundation, 1993), 13.

36. U.S. Bureau of the Census, *Statistical Abstract of the United States 1993*, 113th Edition (U.S. Department of Commerce), 61.

37. David Popenoe, "A New Familism: Renewing Families," *Current* (February 1993): 36.

38. Dr. Richard J. Reif and Gail M. Morse, "Restructuring the Science Classroom," *T.H.E. Journal* (April 1992): 69.

39. Overhead from Press Packet, Farrell Area School District, June 1994.

40. "Student Progress Report," Milwaukee Public Schools, Grand Avenue Middle School, 1991–1992.

41. "Ohio 2000 Discussion Guide," Ohio Department of Education, 1992, 80.

42. Ibid.

43. Handout from a DOE presentation to Ohio State School Board, 1993.

44. John Pierson, "Schools Open Doors To Whole Communities," *Wall Street Journal*, 17 January 1994, B1.

45. Hornbeck and Salamon, *Human Capital*, 380–381.

46. Video taken at Governor's Conference, Kansas.

47. "Cradle-to-Grave" and "Prescription for America" are quoted from photocopies of overheads supplied to authors by Farrell District Area School, June 1994.

48. Phone interview by author with Nancy Hromyak, Farrell School Community Outreach Specialist, 10 September 1994.

49. Pat Crawford, "Supt. Starts Early, Stays With Dropout Prevention Partnership," *Leadership News*, 15 April 1992, 5.

50. Karen S. Peterson, "Schools Add D for Day Care to ABC's," *USA Today*, October 1988, 7.

51. John Hambrose, " 'Partnerships' Vital In This School District," *Scranton Times*, 1 June 1993, 1, 4.

52. Richard Robbins, "Farrell Schools 'Womb to the Tomb,' " *Tribune-Review*, 20 September 1992, A1, A10.

53. Lucy May, "U.S. Education Chief Lauds Kentucky Reform," *Lexington Herald-Leader*, (16 October 1993), C3.

54. Kentucky Education Reform Act of 1990, House Bill 940, Sec. 18.

55. Ibid., Sec. 18(3), (4).

56. Judy Paternostro, letter reprinted in *Kentucky Citizen Digest* (March/April 1993): 3.

57. Ibid., 6.

58. Ibid., 1, 2, 6.

59. Judy Paternostro, letter to Kentucky Centers Task Force, Chairman, 19 April 1991.

60. "Specific Services That May, Under Certain Circumstances, Be Provided Without Parental Consent," Cabinet for Human Resources, n. d.

61. "1993 NEA Resolutions," C-26, "The Association believes that every school district should provide counseling . . . for students who are struggling with their sexual/gender orientation," as quoted in *Education Reporter* (August 1993): 3.

62. Jessica Portner, "Baltimore Plan To Offer Teenagers Norplant Raises Ethical, Medical, Legal Questions," *Education Week* (16 December 1992): 1, 13.

63. *Family Planning Perspectives*, vol. 23, no. 1 (January/February 1991): 15.

64. Paternostro, letter to Kentucky Centers.

65. "GOALS 2000 Community Update," (U.S. Department of Education, December 1993/January 1994), 1.

66. "Alabama Gap Analysis: Developing a Blueprint for Reform," 43. Although the document only has a title, it was written under the guidance of David Hornbeck and published by A+ in 1992.

67. Letter from Kentucky Rep. Thomas R. Kerr, 7 October 1993.

68. "Blueprint For School Transformation, Iowa K-12, Education Reform Study Committee," (Legislative Service Bureau, January 1993), 25.

69. 1993 NEA Resolutions include "public school for children birth through age eight" (B-1); "health, social and psychological services within . . . school" (C-22); "community-operated, school-based family planning clinics" (I-13), as cited in *Education Reporter* (August 1993): 3, 4.

70. "GOALS 2000 Community Update," (U.S. Department of Education, July/August 1994).

71. "Integration of Social Services Task Force Report: for Oregon's H.B. 3565," Oregon Department of Education, (January 1993): 6.

72. Ibid.

73. "Middle Level Task Force Report: for Oregon's H.B. 3565" (January 1993), 16.

74. Ira Magaziner, chair, *America's Choice: high skills or low wages! The Report of the Commission on the Skills of the American Work Force* (Rochester, New York: National Center on Education and the Economy, June 1990), 75.

75. Ibid., 73.

76. Ann Bradley, "Teachers' Report Envisions Radically New Future for Schools," *Education Week* (20 March 1991).

77. *Together We Can* (U.S. Department of Education and U.S. Department of Health and Human Service, April 1993), vii.

78. "GOALS 2000 Community Update" (U.S. Department of Education, September 1993).

79. *Together We Can*, 13.

80. "Briefing Book: Ohio Family & Children First Initiative" (Office of the Governor, 1992), 4.

81. Ibid., 5.

82. Ibid.

83. "Removing the Barriers: Unleashing Ohio's Learning Power" (draft) (Ohio Department of Education with Ohio's Governor's Office, 4 December 1992).

84. According to *Legislative Update* (Ohio Home Education Council, May/June 1993).

85. Phone interview by author with council member (name withheld), 5 August 1994.

86. *Together We Can*, 78.

87. Ibid., 89.

88. Hornbeck and Salamon, *Human Capital*, 380–381.

89. "The Swedish Model," Review and Outlook, *Wall Street Journal*, 7 April 1992, A16.

90. William Shirer, *The Rise and Fall of the Third Reich* (New York: Simon and Schuster, 1959), 249.

SEVEN

TOURING AN OBE CLASSROOM

*There is learning [know], there is understanding [do],
and there is acceptance [be like]. After Winston's reeducation in the Ministry of Love, without a pause he
wrote . . . TWO AND TWO MAKE FIVE.*
—George Orwell, *1984*

Touring an OBE School (Learning Center)

Please join our tour of an outcome-based education
school. Our guidebook will be a 1993 article from an OBE
publication, "The High Success Connection: A Newsletter
for Implementors of Transformational Outcome-Based
Education."

Welcome to the town of Charterville, "A Total Community of Learners," where OBE "literally restructured everything that used to be called 'school.'" Now school is the
learning center, and youngsters are labeled "learners" and
"co-teachers" (formerly called students, they often teach
younger children). They also coach each other, realizing
that "learning teams will be prepared to teach other teams
what they have learned." Emphasis is placed on group learning, student tutoring, and using calculators and computers.

Learners direct teacher/parent conferences—portfolios
are presented to parents by their children, not the teacher.
And, students exit school by completing "graduation demonstrations."

Traditional learning is often ridiculed. Children "laugh
as they recall the twenty words they had to memorize for

the weekly spelling test" and "dissolve into laughter about . . . how things have changed from when they just read books and memorized facts."

Saturday classes are normal. Year-round school is beginning. "Walls between many classrooms have been removed." In fact, the town becomes like a classroom, where groups of learners walk in clusters up and down the streets carrying lap-top computers.

Business partnerships and apprenticeships are integral to OBE. A store window displays an "Experts Wanted" banner encouraging volunteers for the expansion of business/education partnerships.

In the bank, one learning team waits for an interview with the loan manager. They plan to start a health-conscious cookie business that will enable them to buy an acre of rain forest. This "group of four learners begins to noisily examine some of the furniture in the bank." They suspect it's teak, an endangered hardwood from the rain forest in Brazil. "They wonder aloud if that means they should go to another bank for the loan."

"Though the town is fictional," explains author Kit Marshall, "the descriptions are absolutely real—each instance is a report of an authentic example."[1]

New Classroom, New Emphasis, New Outcomes

Notice that the above vignette never mentioned improved reading, ability grouping, or individual achievement. Children ridiculed traditional education—memorizing facts and reading books. Instead, OBE's new classroom (learning center) emphasized the academically soft (but politically correct) "new basics" like cooperation and environmental awareness. One team of learners indignantly sniffed out environmental "crimes" at a local bank.

As discussed in previous chapters, OBE means shaping attitudes, beliefs, and behaviors (political, spiritual, environmental, sexual, and cultural) to meet state-desired standards. These standards are called *outcomes*.

All curriculum, all classroom activities, all advancement of students, *everything* must revolve around outcomes.[2] In

Pennsylvania, outcomes, not Carnegie Units, now determine who will graduate. And, like dominos, all states are lined up to fall quietly under OBE's spell. (Recently a few states jumped out of that line.[3]) Confident OBE evangelists like Dr. Spady say history may remember Pennsylvania as the state that "launched the new revolution in American schools."[4]

OBE's revolution turns traditional classrooms upside-down: 1) Teachers become coaches because children are cooperative group learners; 2) Textbooks (reading is "passive") are thrown out when computers (computer learning is "active") are brought in; 3) Facts are replaced by politically correct outcomes.

Keystone State outcomes require that all students demonstrate:

- cooperating with others

- an understanding of the ethical impact of science on future life

- an understanding of the history and nature of prejudice and relating them to current issues[5]

Who Controls Classroom Content?

At Pennsylvania OBE informational town meetings, citizens stood up and asked, "But what if we don't agree with certain outcomes? Can we opt our children out of them?" The state's answer was always, "No."

Does this sound like local control? Who controls a child's classroom content—parent or state? With OBE, the state prevails.

Today, all fifty-three outcomes in Pennsylvania are mandated from the capitol at Harrisburg down to the individual child in his classroom. Pro-OBE Department of Education bureaucrats believe they can't trust today's family to teach proper values; but the government *can* be trusted. So, law mandates that students learn government values (outcomes) in class. Is that a good idea? Would it be okay if those outcomes were values whose definition everyone agreed on, like "freedom"? During an OBE debate, a state official asked, "Don't you want us to make your children believe democracy is better than totalitarianism?"

"No," a mother of five answered firmly. "I want classes to *teach* that democracy is better than totalitarianism. But, once you *mandate* my child *believe* it, that is totalitarianism."

Modeling vs. Mandating

What's one difference between a traditional classroom and an outcome-based class? One teaches ideas; the other mandates that a child demonstrate he accepts those ideas.

The battle against OBE is sometimes stereotyped as fundamentalists trying to superimpose their Christian values on the public school. That's not the issue. The fight isn't over classes teaching ideas and values. Parents opposing restructuring want positive values modeled in each class. Children need ethics reinforced, but citizens strongly object to values becoming academic subjects. Then, who will define values? Who will determine a standard of mastery? Who will grade prejudice? Cooperation? Honesty? Self-esteem? Understanding self? Adaptability to change? Environmental responsibility? Will the parent or the state define these values?

The OBE controversy is not a religious issue; it's a battle over a child's freedom to think independently. That's a civil rights issue.

A familiar question recurs, *"Is classroom OBE concerned with teaching academics or changing values?"*

Cooperative Learners (Workers)

Let's step back into Kit Marshall's OBE learning center (classroom) for a moment. We observe that students are labeled "co-teachers." They coach each other; students tutor one another; and they learn in groups. OBE literature strongly advocates "cooperative learning (to foster learning success for all)."[6]

Individualism, a value which Americans prize so highly, is completely overshadowed by the state's new value—collectivism. Everybody is equal. Group think. Everyone within a group must cooperate.

For years, cooperative learning has been a successful tool. It was used as one among many teaching methods and carefully supervised. Although schools should encourage students to work well with peers, OBE assesses group cooperation and grades it. Cooperating with others even becomes a requirement for graduation when it appears as an outcome, as it does in Pennsylvania.

"Works cooperatively with others"[7] is included in the *SCANS* list of workplace competencies. Therefore, all states' outcomes may include it. You can also look for it when the national performance standards (outcomes) are unveiled.

Besides outcomes, collective cooperation pops up in three activities: 1) ability grouping; 2) cooperative learning; 3) peer tutoring.

Ability Grouping

OBE eliminates tracking (grouping children according to ability). Why? Because equality of opportunity is more important than academic success. "Gifted" students lose enrichment programs. Honors courses disappear. "I fear academic leveling will occur," high school English teacher Linda Young told the Colorado Senate Education Committee.[8] Her school already eliminated ninth grade honors English. (Interestingly, when Young openly spoke against OBE, she received her first poor evaluation in more than twenty years of teaching—she was being an individualist, not a "cooperative worker.")[9]

Cooperative Learning

Remember, OBE says cooperative learning is to foster learning success for all. But, what do students themselves say? A study published in *Education Leadership* revealed that gifted kids resent mixed-ability group learning. Frustrated, bright children don't know how to motivate other children. And, although ambitious students do a lion's share of the work, they receive the lazy group's low grade.[10] Cooperative grading makes them feel intellectually abused.

As a mandated outcome, cooperating in groups also may include playing together:

Kent rushed home from his OBE school and burst into tears. His third grade class cooperation exercise had been to role-play settlers on the Oregon Trail. His teacher told each wagon leader to assign fellow students some disease or injury. Kent's group boss gave him the "disease" of muteness to shut him up. You see, Kent is a happy, talkative student, but he's partially deaf and has a speech impediment. Bewildered and hurt, Kent said, "I quit. I don't want to play." He was graded "F" in cooperative learning.[11]

Peer Tutoring

Group cooperation also means peer tutoring. In the same Pennsylvania OBE classroom, third-grader Peter, who is a math whiz, complains he's bored. He wants to learn more math. Although he masters his assignments quickly, Peter must tutor his classmates; he isn't allowed to work ahead. For Peter, "success for all" means learning at a snail's pace. The entire class, with its special education students, moves through each unit at the same rate.[12]

Peter's parents say they don't send him to school to be the teacher. His mother explains, "Peter attends school to be a student. If he's teaching someone else math he already knows, then he isn't learning a new math concept himself, is he?"

But, Does it Work?

A 1987 Johns Hopkins University research report called it a "Robin Hood" approach.[13] Cooperative, group-based mastery learning takes "time away from high achievers to increase it for low achievers."[14] The report also found that OBE's mastery learning is an academic "leveling process."[15]

With OBE, children retake tests without penalty until reaching mastery (80 percent or better). OBE's magazine, *Outcomes*, says one of the nine standards for OBE is that when grading, teachers must throw away their pens and "replace them with pencils that have large erasers."[16] Physics teachers in Boyertown, Pennsylvania, sent a memo to all parents saying that although they had hoped students would learn more, OBE/mastery learning "simply did not work."

Teachers explained that students were "milking the system." Pupils figured out they could take the test, flunk it (while getting a long look at the questions), get tutored, then easily pass the exam. Teachers soon discontinued using it.[17]

Cindy Morgan, a high schooler from Fremont, California, says of OBE's cooperative learning, "Most of the time one person ends up doing all the work, and everybody gets the credit." Do students learn teamwork or social skills? Just the opposite. Cindy says, "People who aren't doing anything are learning to mooch."[18]

OBE sells itself as a world-class education preparing future workers, yet it states there are no deadlines and no consequences if you don't do it right the first time. Group cooperation is vital to equality, but it eclipses individualism. Is good work-force education removing youngsters from reality? Just ask a surgeon, an assembly worker, or a pilot if their jobs require calendars and clocks. Ask them if there are consequences if they don't get it right the first time. George Washington Carver turned the peanut into soap, ink, and three hundred other productive uses because he wasn't afraid to explore apart from the group.

A familiar question recurs, *"Is classroom OBE concerned with teaching academics or changing values?"*

Cooperating with Others: What's the State's Definition?

Is the state molding future workers who will cooperatively (obediently) change jobs? Workers who will follow the group? Workers who will comply with the group's ethics?

Let's look at another real classroom. It's 1987. Students busily pencil in test bubbles. They're taking a state assessment test called Pennsylvania Educational Quality Assessment (EQA). Among other things, it measures a child's "willingness to honor self-made commitments to . . . groups."[19] Here are some questions:[20]

A person in a crowd is standing on a street corner. They are protesting about something. Some people pick up rocks and start throwing them at windows. I would ALSO THROW ROCKS when I knew: [a] There was no chance of getting caught, [b] I agreed with what they were protesting about, [c] My closest friend decided to throw rocks.

The principal invites an unpopular political speaker to the school. The speaker has ideas that most students strongly disagree with. A group of students decide to shout the speaker down. In this situation I would HELP SHOUT THE SPEAKER DOWN when I knew: [a] I didn't agree with the speaker's ideas, [b] The speaker said he didn't respect student ideas, [c] The principal had refused to let the speaker we liked talk to us.

There is a secret club at school called the Midnight Artists. They go out late at night and paint funny sayings and pictures on buildings. A student is asked to join the club. In this situation, I would JOIN THE CLUB when I knew: [a] My best friend asked me to join, [b] The most popular students were in the club, [c] My parents would ground me if they found out I joined.

Many students look for an answer that fits their traditional values such as "I would *not* break windows with rocks" (Isn't that violent protesting?); or "I would *not* shout down a speaker" (Isn't that disrespectful?). They find none. Teenagers wonder why, in the state assessment, those Judeo/Christian ethics aren't an option.

By the way, the correct answers to our last EQA question about the Midnight Artists are: [a] yes, [b] yes, [c] no.[21]

The only "appropriate" answers on the state EQA test appear to be those indicative of a "conformist mentality," observes a 1993 *Education Week* article. The piece warns, "Most states use similar tests."[22]

This assessment tested a child's belief system. It measured "locus of control." Do outside influences motivate behavior, or is the child internally driven?[23] And, it scored attitudes about cooperatively going along with the crowd. The preferred answers showed a willingness to conform to group goals (even if that meant denying one's personal beliefs).

High school student Garrett Hoge didn't like having his personal beliefs assessed, so he showed his parents a few questions he had quickly scribbled on a scrap of paper during the EQA test. Queries such as: "The prospect of working most of my adult life depresses me—'yes,' 'no,' or 'sometimes.' "

Irate, the Hoges spent several years exposing the truth about the EQA. Subsequently, it was exchanged for another state assessment. Otherwise it would still be "providing data . . . for curriculum"[24] in that state. Nevertheless, the former head of that EQA testing program, in the 1994 article "A New World Order: The Goal of Outcome Based Education? A Response," implied that other states are following in that assessment's footsteps. He bragged that the "EQA was ahead of its time."[25] Just as on the EQA, might attitudes such as willingness to cooperate be assessed by other states?

What are the state's definitions of outcomes like "cooperating with others"? If it's not individualism, is it bowing to consensus?

Think about a shy, lone wolf, gifted student in English class who refuses to participate in collaborative writing groups. What will happen to future Ernest Hemingways?

Again we must ask, *"Is classroom OBE concerned with teaching academics or changing values?"*

Teacher as Coach: Machine as Instructor

"Lecture is a dirty word as we focus ever more on 'cooperative learning,' " laments high school teacher Linda Young.[26] Students are now tutors and cooperative learners. That's why this chapter's opening story calls children "co-teachers." Do you know what happens then to the adult teacher's role?

Teachers become coaches. Kentucky now says, "The teacher is a 'coach.' "[27] Ohio OBE restructurers see the "teacher as mentor, coach, learning facilitator."[28] In fact, "teacher-as-coach" is one of nine principles required in education's swiftly spreading outcomes-based model called Re:Learning—Theodore Sizer's "OBE" model (mentioned in chapter 1). Part of Sizer's design recommends, "Do not waste class time on 'teaching.' Class time can be better spent with students working collaboratively."[29] (Re:Learning's 1989-1990 National Advisory Board included two familiar names, Ira Magaziner and Bill Clinton).[30]

Throughout our discussion, you've seen the impact of the Department of Labor's *SCANS* manual. (Remember? *SCANS* relied on Ira Magaziner and Hillary Rodham Clinton's *America's Choice* report.) According to *SCANS*, because of emerging technologies, "teachers and students will change their traditional roles."[31] Teachers should coach and facilitate while machines instruct. That's right. Technology will "dispense information" and "monitor learning."[32]

Skinnerian Conditioning

Behavioral psychologist B. F. Skinner once wrote, "What we need is a technology of behavior"[33]—a systematic and scientific program to alter the nature of man.[34] And, Skinner called educational computers "teaching machines."[35]

According to a 1983 *Education Week* interview with Skinner, his behavioral conditioning theories were "instrumental in the development of mastery learning [OBE] and the 'teaching machines.' "[36] Skinner's controversial plan was to modify behavior using individualized instruction[37] and technology.

Pennsylvania's Daniel Boone Junior High School uses a manual called "Academic/Behavior Modification." On page one, the first premise is, "A person is basically good."[38] Although this belief statement is inconsistent with Judeo/Christian beliefs, it's in total alignment with the *Humanist Manifesto II*, which B.F. Skinner enthusiastically signed. He preached that environment can condition moral behavior since "man is not a moral animal."[39]

OBE embraces Skinner's behavioral engineering method. His "teaching machine," using a stimulus-response-stimulus process, will recycle children until they meet all the outcomes.

Learning Nuggets

Keep in mind OBE's value-laden outcomes like cooperation, diversity, environmentalism, and self-esteem. Today, educators see computers as ideal for changing a child's attitudes. "The computer is ideally suited to the role of facilitator in values education," says the *Education Leadership* article "Can Computers Teach Values?"[40]

Consider the position statement of Pennsylvania administrators on classroom technology: The computer individualized programs will "improve personalization and humanization of learning."[41] Why call teachers (humans) "coaches," and computers (machines) "personal and human teachers"?

The OBE class, with retesting and moving pupils at individual paces, can't afford a teacher for each student. So, there must be a plan.

A proposed solution is called Computer Assisted Instruction. Each child will be tied in to a computer. Programs will be individualized, and the computer will serve up "Learning Nuggets." In order to create individual lesson plans, the computer will access "biographical data, learning styles, assessment criteria, etc." on each student.[42]

The Learning Nugget will access your child's background, his beliefs, and how he learns. That's "learning style." Then, it must search for the most effective way to change behavior, to attack attitudes and serve it back up to the child.

Here's Lookin' at You—Federal Data Banks

Where does the computer find learning data and biographical files? Who has access to such personal information?

Gathering Learning Data and Biographical Files

A coalition of Pennsylvania parents discovered that some states, including their own, are starting to compile data banks at a microrecord level (i.e., on individual children).[43] For example, Ohio, since 1991, has been collecting ninety-three categories of personal information on each student.[44] Meanwhile, Massachusetts 1993 Reform Act requires each school district to "maintain individual records on every student and employee . . . and such other information as the department shall determine necessary."[45]

The federal government wants each state to collect copious amounts of the same comprehensive data on students. Pennsylvania parents read in the *Wall Street Journal* that the National Education Goals Panel recommended that "schools start collecting reams of new information on individual students."[46] According to government sources, that data would come from both public and private schools.[47]

Parents wondered, was the federal government harvesting private information which could program a Learning Nugget, or, as B. F. Skinner aptly stated, "shape behavior as a sculptor shapes a lump of clay"?[48] Concern increased when these coalition members uncovered the federal data bank.

Federal Data Bank

They saw in one of ten federal data handbooks a page listing "Major Categories of Student Information." Individual codes specified "name, student number, family responsibilities, family economic information, oral health [including "number of teeth decayed"]."[49] Plus, "medical history [Did you have any surgery? Did you ever abuse drugs?], school performance, non-school performance [What are your non-school activities?]," your "mental" and "psychological characteristics" and your "most effective learning style."[50]

A little graph in another data handbook showed these coalition members how all coded data on the child could be linked. It connected the child to detailed information about a teacher, which linked teacher and child to data on the curriculum—all at an individual level.[51]

Puzzle pieces could easily fit together to make a complete picture of a Learning Nugget. One parent shuddered.

He whispered, "So, if the state wants to change my second grader's behavior, it can change his teacher, his textbook, or, the state can remediate him using a customized Nugget."

"First you call teacher 'a coach,' effectively removing the classroom authority figure—with an individual personality," another parent reflected out loud. "Then, to replace the teacher, you substitute group learning and machines. Plus, everything is programmed to help students meet the same politically correct, attitudinal outcomes. Doesn't that create group think? Sameness? Collectivism? No individuality?"

Federal Connection?

Is the state really collecting personal data on students and their families? Schools try to calm worried parents by saying that personal information gathered in the classroom won't be transferred out of the district without parents' approval. But, Orange County, California, school board member Tom Chaffee might disagree. He was irate when, in 1994, one thousand students took a federal student survey, without parental knowledge or consent. The questions were non-academic, many related to family relationships:[52]

1) I don't want my parents to help me.

2) My parents don't understand my homework well enough to help me.

3) My parents don't have the time to help me.

4) My parents don't want to help me.

One section sounded like a psychological profile:

i) I certainly feel useless at times.

m) Chance and luck are very important for what happens in my life.

j) At times I think I am no good at all.

The questionnaire required a student's name and phone number as well as a list of relatives' names and addresses.

It even had a bar code. Was the government just gathering aggregate data to examine trends? If so, why require names and addresses?

The Pennsylvania Coalition wanted to know, "Is the federal government tracking children today?" They soon found out. Researchers in the group examined a copy of their state's federal "Guidelines and Application for the Drug-Free Schools and Community Act of 1986." (All states' federal guidelines are similar.) They learned that accepting federal grant money for this program required schools to provide programs for decision making and self-esteem, plus psychological services.

But, what made them speechless was the list of little codes to the left of the services required. Each code exactly matched the codes in one of the federal data bank's handbooks.[53] Were state programs currently sending data to the federal system?

Speedy Delivery (SPEEDE/ExPRESS)

And, watch for Internet, an electronic superhighway—formatted by SPEEDE/ExPRESS—whisking information back and forth.[54]

Your child's resumé will be traveling that electronic highway. Chapter 4 mentioned *SCANS*' resumé of Jane Smith (the nineteen-year-old, graded in honesty, who hadn't gotten her CIM). That report card was a sample showing schools how to format an electronic resumé for "an electronic information system."[55] It included information about Jane's portfolio. Will portfolios be part of the OBE classroom? Yes—if you want to get your Certificate of Initial Mastery.

In one of Oregon's CIM pilot schools, Lakeridge High, pupils were informed that "each student in the state of Oregon is soon going to be required to have a portfolio which contains samples of his/her work. These portfolios will be used to assess students' progress in order to receive a Certificate of Initial Mastery."[56] You will not be able to get your CIM without a portfolio.

What goes into the portfolio? Remember the values appraisal in the beginning of chapter 1, with statements like: "If I ask God for forgiveness, my sins are forgiven" and "I love my parents"? These were to be included in Lakeridge High's student portfolio. At the same time, across the country in Gastonia, North Carolina, students completed the identical values appraisal. A school official informed one parent that it would also go into a portfolio.[57]

Also, the *SCANS* talks about "the Three P's": projects, performance and portfolios.[58] (What happened to evaluation based on the three Rs?)

And This Little "P" Went to the Classroom

One of the three "P's"—portfolio—is a familiar assessment tool in the OBE classrooms. What is an OBE portfolio? Rather than a manila folder lovingly stuffed with your second grader's cute artwork, these are electronic portfolios. They're stuffed with documentation showing that your child is meeting the outcomes.

Listen to a 1993 memo written by Pennsylvania Federation of Teachers union Vice President Jack Steinberg. He not only opposes OBE, but he also specifically objects to OBE's excessive computer use, including the electronic portfolio: "Based on the [OBE] theory that each child works at his/her own speed," Steinberg warns, "each child must be tracked, via computer, to maintain an ongoing record of every evaluation of every child . . . from the moment the student enters school." He states that computers will store "each child's portfolio."[59]

Schools are starting to use computer programs such as the Grady Profile "to create an electronic portfolio."[60]

So What?

So? What's wrong with OBE classrooms using electronic portfolios?

First, portfolios in computers are easily accessed; that's a privacy problem.

Second, portfolios are files that may follow you throughout life; that's a security problem. The *New York Times* reports that China keeps a file, called a *dangan*, on citizens. This file starts in elementary school and "shadows the person throughout life." It moves directly from school to employer. "The dangan [file] contains political evaluations that affect career prospects and permission to leave the country."[61]

When Lan, a recent immigrant from China, heard about electronic portfolios and OBE's politically loaded outcomes, she commented, "In China, everything goes in a file, the *dangan*. My parents told me, 'Don't answer anything wrong [politically] in school.'" Lan continued, "No mistakes get erased. Employers know all your background, attitudes, everything."[62]

Third, portfolios are experimental; that's an academic problem. Because they dovetail with outcome-based assessment, many schools are being pressured into using portfolios. Yet, the nation's *first* portfolio-based field trials didn't begin until fall 1994.[63] And, what happened when Vermont (a state pioneering portfolios) hired Rand Corporation to analyze its portfolio assessment? The Rand study found that, due to inconsistent, subjective scoring, results were unreliable.[64]

Furthermore, computers are expensive; that's a consumer problem. Big business views the classroom with cash registers in its eyes. Education's forty million students are a multibillion dollar market for computer companies.[65] But, like the much-hyped language labs (using tape recorders) of the 1980s, might this computer-as-teacher concept be another expensive joke? Who will benefit most from the proliferation of classroom computers—students or big business?

Portfolios are not new; that's not the problem. Compiling portfolios of students' work in *individual* classrooms isn't new, and it certainly isn't wrong. But, OBE's portfolios will 1) be cumulative files; 2) be graded; 3) be electronic; 4) be filled with personal demonstrations of politically laden outcomes. That's what is wrong.

OBE's History Class: Eroding Nationalism

According to Pete du Pont, former governor of Delaware, outcome-based education "quite literally does everything wrong." He says, "Indeed, it [OBE] fundamentally abdicates teaching of academic knowledge and skills and embraces political indoctrination and social engineering."[66]

International Education

OBE social engineers tell classrooms to produce workers for a global economy. That means children must be educated to think "global village" rather than "nation state." Therefore, in the classroom, international education becomes paramount—stealing time away from American history. That's dangerous. Actually, OBE promoters encourage eliminating history as a separate course.[67] (Oklahoma's outcome-based legislative act eliminated "teaching disloyalty to the American Constitutional system of government" as grounds for dismissing teachers.[68]) Pulitzer Prize winner Arthur Schlesinger, Jr., warns that without memory of its past, a nation becomes disoriented and lost.[69]

Lost is a word Molalla High School U. S. history teacher Frank McNutt might use. He says his OBE school in Oregon tells teachers that textbooks are no longer acceptable, and teachers should throw out individual courses, including U.S. history.[70]

International education classes often speak of "America/ Global Village" in the same breath. They are not synonymous. What happens when needs of our nation-state and desires of the other global village members are incompatible? To survive, U.S. interests must always be served first. OBE outcomes, like "appreciate the mutual dependence of all people in the world,"[71] will erode nationalism.

Yet, the OBE state of Minnesota has a document called *Model Learner Outcomes for International Education*. Its preface includes, "our world has become a global village."[72] This document says international education is integrated into most all classes.[73] In other words, all courses will teach

children global citizenship, and parents can't opt their kids
out. One of Minnesota's Learner Goals (outcomes) is "be a
responsible citizen of the . . . world."[74]

A fifth grade classroom near Pittsburgh has as its over-
all year's theme: "Global Awareness: Our Interdependence,
Our Interconnectedness." Math, science, health, social studies, all subjects are integrated and emphasize that theme.
One outcome in a Colonial Unit is for "groups of students
to develop their own culture."[75] (Again, notice the emphasis
on groups. But, more important, might telling ten-year-olds
to invent their own culture cause them to doubt the supe-
riority of America's heritage?) Global education can undermine the importance of U. S. national sovereignty—did the
colonists write a Declaration of Independence or Interdependence?

How will the OBE emphasis on global studies affect
patriotism? That's what anchorwoman Jayna Davis wanted
Bill Spady to answer during a 1993 television interview at
his home. She asked, "Where do patriotism and nationalism fit into education?"

OBE's guru squirmed slightly and answered, "I don't
know." Ms. Davis pressed, "Do you think a child needs to
learn to be patriotic?" "Maybe," he mumbled. Silence. "I
don't know what 'patriotic' means,"[76] he added.

The Multicultural Express

OBE also force-feeds young children diversity, or
multiculturalism, the grand-sounding names for celebrating
all cultures. Although studying other cultures is praisewor-
thy, multiculturalism is more concerned with political correctness than strong academics.

Because *SCANS* workplace competencies include "works
with cultural diversity,"[77] multiculturalism (also called diversity, appreciating others, etc.) is forced into every state's list
of outcomes. For example, one of Kentucky's seventy-five
outcomes tells students to demonstrate an appreciation for
a multicultural world.[78]

Multiculturalism focuses on two politically correct
themes. First, *all* diverse cultures must be esteemed except

Western culture. To help shape "correct" attitudes, class-room materials may "expand" history to the point of falsi-fying it. For example, school districts in Milwaukee, Pitts-burgh, and Portland use essays that assert blacks in ancient Egypt invented electric batteries and mastered flight with gliders. The coordinator of multicultural education in Port-land also says that Napoleon personally shot off the Sphinx's nose so it wouldn't be recognized as African.[79]

Second, students are instructed to respect ethics from all cultures, except those derived from a Judeo-Christian heritage. In fact, this would constitute "ethnocentrism" of the worst sort: judging right from wrong using The Ten Commandments as your moral guide, for example.

According to a teachers' union publication, "The oppo-site of ethnocentrism—the attitude that diversity seeks to promote—is cultural relativism."[80] That means using Judeo/Christian standards to judge right from wrong in other cultures is bad, but cultural relativism is good—all cultures are morally equal. And, unless you're a religious believer, morality has no objective standard. What's right and wrong changes from culture to culture and must be appreciated.

That's why gay lobbyists from the homosexual "culture" try to get OBE into classrooms. In the name of diversity, children should appreciate homosexuality. Study it. Con-sider it. Give gay "diversity" equal time in sex education instruction.

"Help us [through OBE] to educate those who are so vastly uneducated in the meaning of the word diversity,"[81] said Scott Tyson. At a hearing to mandate OBE in his state, Tyson testified in behalf of a lesbian and gay outreach association. He stressed that OBE will "remove the moral and religious blinders that so often hinder our [gay] ad-vances."[82] What's to stop the pedophile culture from de-manding the same thing?

Florida's outcome-based act, Blueprint 2000, was fol-lowed by a state directive telling schools to teach multiculturalism. Its purpose is "to eliminate personal and national ethnocentrism so that children understand that a specific culture is not intrinsically superior or inferior to any other."[83] Does that make academic sense? European explorers arrived here and encountered an Aztec culture which had no alphabet or wheel and practiced human sacrifice. Are children really to be taught that *all* cultures are intellectually and morally equal?

Exactly. When Florida's Lake County school board added an amendment saying America's culture is "unquestionably superior,"[84] the teachers' union filed a lawsuit to overturn the local board's decision.

This is the Lake County amendment that caused such an uproar:

> [Instruction] shall also include and instill in our students an appreciation of our American heritage and culture such as: our republican form of government, capitalism, a free-enterprise system, patriotism, strong family values, freedom of religion and other basic values that are superior to other foreign or historic cultures.[85]

OBE's focus is on egalitarianism—equality of all nations, all cultures, all ethics—not on academics.

In one OBE school, during a multicultural course dealing with India, the teacher darkened the room, flicked on the overhead projector and told ninth graders, "Empty your minds. Focus on the light [from the projector]. And meditate." OBE goes beyond what a student must *know* (knowledge about India); it requires students to *do* (practice Hindu meditation); and *be like* (become a multicultural citizen).

Again, *Is classroom OBE concerned with teaching academics or changing values?*

Kiss Facts Goodbye

To reach the numerous non-academic outcomes, America's tried and true traditional education must disappear. Did you notice in this chapter's first section, "A Total Community of Learners," OBE students twice laughed at memorizing spelling words and memorizing facts?

OBE reformers viciously attack drilling and memorizing. That sets up a straw man—traditional education. Classic education is stereotyped as doing little more than dishing out facts. That's one reason why the Littleton, Colorado, high school principal, mentioned in chapter 1, refused to agree that every graduate should know something about the Holocaust. Using restructuring's rhetoric, he explained, "A curriculum that includes specific facts is outdated in a changing world."[86]

Denigrating knowledge by portraying it as nothing but learning facts is unfair. Facts are the mortar for knowledge. Think back to your favorite history teachers. They taught you specific dates, places, and names, then cemented those facts with trends and ideas and gave you knowledge.

Why Learn Facts in an "Information Age"?

The OBE idea is that Industrial Age education must give way to Information Age teaching. They say facts multiply so quickly today, we shouldn't stuff them into our children's brains. Sound logical? Not if you believe academics are important. For one thing, basic facts never change.

Today's shift from teaching facts leads to horror stories shared among professors. At University of California at Berkeley, a history professor says students often are unable to differentiate between the American Revolution and the Civil War.[87]

Without memorizing facts, how will children spell irregular words? (Even computer spell checkers aren't infallible—that explains why, in 1992, the Associated Press misspelled *accommodate* sixty-nine times.[88]) Without memorizing, how will little ones learn the alphabet? (One teacher in Cleveland was told to take down the alphabet letters bordering her room because memorizing the alphabet would confuse children while they learned whole language.) Would OBE promoters ridicule memorizing math facts, a Shakespeare sonnet, or the Gettysburg Address? Without facts, knowledge becomes mere opinion.

Japan consistently outscores most countries, including the United States, on international tests. Their secret? According to a recent worldwide study, Japan does *not* use subjective performance-based assessments (like portfolios), and "rote memorization of facts is the norm."[89] The world's most effective secondary schools rely heavily on drilling and memorizing facts. Does that surprise you?

It doesn't surprise children in Houston, Texas, at the much publicized Wesley School. For instance, in a typical first grade class, a teacher, Earlene Alexander, works with about ten children on phonics, reading, and spelling drills. Simultaneously, the rest of the class copies words over and over. That's memorizing alphabet sounds and rote drilling—dusty old Industrial Age education, right? And, in this classroom, 95 percent are Afro-American students (with 85 percent qualifying for free lunches). Yet, last year, Alexander's first-grade class was reading on a fifth-grade level.[90] That's a fact, not an opinion.

What's Cookin?

But, OBE doesn't allow such "facts" to impede its quest to transform every classroom in America. Transformational OBE must totally break the mold of the traditional classroom. That means smashing traditional education, which was based on Western Judeo/Christian principles. Restructured schools are built on faddish interpretations of secular humanism. (Environment determines behavior, and man is perfectible, if trained properly.)

A U.S. representative from Texas, Dick Armey, doesn't mince words: "Just what is OBE? Boil away all the rhetoric about 'world class standards,' etc., and it's simply the behaviorist teaching of B.F. Skinner applied to education." Representative Armey continues, "It [OBE] weans children from their parents' values to instill in them politically correct, secular-left values."[91]

Social engineers believe the transformational OBE school is a child's utopia. But, others say it's the government's pot intended to slowly boil frogs. Put frogs in boiling water, and they'll jump right out. But put them in cold water, then slowly turn up the heat; shortly you'll have boiled frogs— politically correct, cooperative workers.

Is Your School Becoming Frog Soup?

By the year 2000, throughout America, the water is scheduled to be at a rolling boil. During the late 1980s and early 1990s, few saw OBE's federal connections. Many well-intentioned administrators incorporated OBE locally, while misled state legislators began passing OBE legislation state-wide. Neither saw the larger picture.

For instance, Michigan passed outcome-based education in 1993. At the time, it appeared to be simply another innovative approach to education. "We approved outcome-based education without seeing the full picture," admits Michigan State Sen. Gilbert J. Dinello. "That full picture is now becoming clearer with the state being targeted to assume the role of nurturer, as well as educator of our children. The programming of little minds will take place."[92]

Will the state's opinion become more important than facts? Will your child have to compile a portfolio in order to get a CIM? Will the acceptance of global citizenship be important? Will appreciating diverse cultures be graded? What will be stored in data banks? Will 2+2 = 5, if the state says it does?

Again, we wonder, "*Is classroom OBE concerned with teaching academics or changing values?*"

Does your school have OBE? Are your classrooms becoming frog soup? Michigan Alliance of Families, a group monitoring OBE for many years, compiled a guide to help parents find the answer for themselves. (If your school has more than six facets, be suspicious.)

The ABCs of OBE

Does your school have OBE? Do you have:

A. A mission or belief statement which includes "ALL CHILDREN CAN LEARN"

B. A three- to five-year Improvement Plan

C. An Annual Report issued at district and building levels

D. Site-based management. Have your teachers and parents been empowered by serving on hand-picked committees to develop a mission statement or a three- to five-year Improvement or Strategic Plan?

E. Competition de-emphasized

F. Multiage grouping, initially eliminating grades K-3

G. Letter grades *A-B-C-D-E-F* (Bell Curve) replaced with *A-B-I* (*J* Curve), or no letter grading system

H. Outcomes which must be demonstrated, replacing the Carnegie Units (specific requirements for graduation)

I. Inclusive education (mainstreaming of special education and juvenile delinquents into regular classroom)

J. An extended school year (200 days or more) to year-round school; extended class blocks, fewer courses ("Less is more.")

K. Thematic teaching (over a certain length of time, all classes teach to the same theme)

L. Team teaching

M. Cooperative learning and group grades, as well as the elimination of valedictorian or salutatorian

N. De-emphasis of rote memorization of facts and knowledge (content) which are replaced with realistic and relevant teaching

O. Teachers referred to as facilitators or coaches

P. Teaching staff continually involved in professional development designed to train them in consensus building and collaboration

Q. Frequent references to Spady, Hornbeck, Sizer, Goodlad, etc.

R. Certificates proving mastery, awarded at about age 16, followed by a Certificate of Advanced Mastery

S. Individual Education Plans (IEP's) for everyone, or Child Centered Education

T. Continual assessment of growth and development

U. Collaboration and consensus as a goal of all committees

V. Portfolios

W. Higher order thinking skills (HOTS) or critical thinking and the use of Bloom's Taxonomy (Application, Analysis, Synthesis, Evaluation)

X. Partnerships between the school and parents, community, business

Y. Social services linking the school with all community service agencies to become a "one-stop service provider"

Z. Mastery Learning, Performance-Based Education, Glasser's Reality Therapy, Management by Objectives (MBO), Total Quality Management (TQM), Accelerated Schools, Effective Schools, Comer Schools, Schools for the 21st Century, Sizer's Coalition of Essential Schools, Outcomes Driven Developmental Model (ODDM)—all of which are outcome-based education.[93]

Most of the elements mentioned in Michigan's ABCs of OBE were spelled out in Spady's Far West 1984 grant proposal to make OBE a national movement.

Back to the Future

Let's step back into this chapter's make-believe OBE school. We saw students carrying lap-top computers as they ridiculed memorizing. Children also dissolved into laughter remembering when they "just read books."

Similarities with the true-life Saturn School are striking. This Minneapolis school has been cited as a "break-the-mold" model. Saturn's classrooms provide a computer-based, personal plan for each child. According to a 1992 educational journal, "Saturn has no grades or marks; we rely on student portfolios. . . . Because of the . . . 'passivity of textbooks' students almost never use them; learning is meant to be active, 'hands-on'. . . . More often than not they work in cooperative groups, helping and learning from one another. . . . Students use the community for learning. . . . "*94

"A dictum at Saturn: 'Learners will inherit the earth.' "95 Or, will OBE make children inherit the wind?

Endnotes

1. Kit Marshall, "Welcome To Charterville: A Total Community of Learners," *The High Success Connection* (April 1993): 6–10.

2. William G. Spady, "It's Time To Take a Close Look at Outcome-Based Education," *Outcomes* (Summer 1992): 7.

3. Dedicated citizens and alarmed legislators fought hard to halt OBE statewide legislative initiatives in Alabama, Connecticut, Iowa, and Virginia—at least temporarily.

4. "Pa. Reforms in Education Could Send Big Message," *Washington Observer*, 14 March 1993, A2.

5. Adapted from the "Regulations of the State Board of Education of Pennsylvania: Chapter 5 Curriculum," Pennsylvania Department of Education, 31 March 1993, 12.

6. William G. Spady and Kit J. Marshall, "Transformational Outcome-based Education" (1991): 3. (A draft prepared for the October 1991 issue of *Educational Leadership*.)

7. *Learning A Living: A Blueprint for High Performance, A SCANS Report for America 2000*, (U. S. Department of Labor, April 1992), 81.

8. Linda Young, written testimony presented to the Colorado Senate Education Committee, 6 June 1993.

---

*NOTE: Saturn's scores dropped each of the three times its students took the standardized tests in math, reading, and language. Since the school had opened two years before, officials worried, "Saturn's lack of emphasis on basic skills may be handicapping its students" (*Minneapolis-St. Paul Tribune*).96

9. Berry Morson, "Vocal Teacher Given Poor Evaluation," *Rocky Mountain News*, 10 January 1993, 1.

10. Marian Matthews, "Gifted Students Talk about Cooperative Learning," *Educational Leadership* (April 1992): 48–50.

11. Interview by author with Kent and his father, 20 August 1994.

12. Interview by author with Peter's mother, 2 September 1994.

13. Robert E. Slavin, "Mastery Learning Reconsidered," Center for Research on Elementary & Middle Schools, Johns Hopkins University, January 1987, 7.

14. Ibid.

15. Ibid.

16. "The Criteria for Outcome-Based Education," *Outcomes* (Spring 1991): 35.

17. Memo from Boyertown, Pa., physics teachers to physics students and their parents, 16 November 1992.

18. Joanne Jacobs, "New Trend Fails Top Students," *The Oregonian*, 13 May, 1994.

19. *Getting Inside the EQA Inventory*, Pennsylvania Department of Education, 1975, 20.

20. *Pennsylvania Student Questionnaire*, Grade 11, Pennsylvania Department of Education, 1987, 19. Pennsylvania Educational Quality Assessment test.

21. *EQA Inventory*, 20. "Subscale 3: . . .honor self-made commitments to individuals or groups," but avoid punishment.

22. B. K. Eakman, "It's About Mental Health, Stupid: Much That Passes for Education Reform Is Merely 'Psych-Behavioral Calisthenics,' " *Education Week* (20 October 1993): 40

23. *EQA Inventory*, 9. Scoring the EQA.

24. *Pennsylvania Health Assessment Handbook*, Department of Education, 1990, 1.

25. J. Robert Coldiron, "A New World Order: The Goal of Outcome Based Education? A Response," *Pennsylvania Educational Leadership* (Spring 1994): 10.

26. Linda Young, "Teacher Doubts Direction 2000 Effects," *Littleton Independent*, 2 April 1993, 9, 36.

27. *Kentucky Task Force on High School Restructuring Preliminary Draft Report*, a manual from Department of Education, 9 February 1993, 14.

28. "Ohio 2000 Discussion Guide," Ohio Department of Education, 1992, 80.

29. Alan Gartner and Dorothy Kerzner Lipsky, *The Yoke of Special Education: How To Break It* (Rochester, N.Y.: National Center on Education and the Economy, 1989), 28.

30. "Re:Learning in New Mexico: A Focus on Student Success," an undated brochure, 9, and "Prospectus," Coalition of Essential Schools, Brown University, 2. In 1994, the Annenberg Foundation donated $50 million to Theodore Sizer's organization.

31. *SCANS,* xvii.

32. Ibid., xvii.

33. B. F. Skinner, *Beyond Freedom and Dignity* (New York: Vintage Books, 1972), 3.

34. Ibid., first inside page.

35. Susan Walton, "There Has Been a Conspiracy of Silence about Teaching," *Education Week* (31 August 1983): 5.

36. Ibid.

37. Ibid.

38. *Academic/Behavior Modification*, Daniel Boone Junior High School, n. d., 1.

39. Skinner, *Beyond Freedom and Dignity*, 188.

40. Joseph A. Braun, Jr., and Kurt A. Slobodzian, "Can Computers Teach Values?" *Educational Leadership* (April 1982): 509.

41. "Education & Technology: A Position Statement," The Pennsylvania Association for Supervision and Curriculum Development, n. d., 2.

42. "Center for the New West Learning Community Proposal," Figure 1, Grant proposal, n.d., E3.

43. "Micro Record format—all data must be collected and stored in micro record format, with a micro record being defined as a datum on an individual person or an individual entity." Quoted from "Alternatives for a National Data System On Elementary and Secondary Education," U.S. Department of Education (20 December 1985), 60.

44. Alan D. Miller, "Student 'Dossiers' Slammed: Lawmaker Wants Limit on Collection of Data by State," *Columbus Dispatch*, 23 February 93, B1.

45. Massachusetts Education Reform Act of 1993, SB No. 1551, 30.

46. Rochelle Sharpe, "Panel To Suggest U.S. Schools Collect More Comprehensive Data on Students," *Wall Street Journal*, 12 April 1993, A4.

47. "Education Data System Implementation Project," Council of Chief State School Officers, position paper, n.d., 1.

48. B. F. Skinner, *Science and Human Behavior* (London: Collier-MacMillian, 1953), 91.

49. *Handbook V: Student/Pupil Accounting: Standard Terminology and Guide for Managing Student Data in Elementary and Secondary Schools, Community/Junior Colleges, and Adult Education* (Washington, D. C.: National Center for Education, Statistics Education Division, 1976), 45.

50. Ibid., 4.

51. *Handbook III, Elementary and Secondary Education Property Accounting: A Handbook of Standard Terminology and a Guide For Classifying Information about Education Property* (Washington, D. C.: National Center for Education Statistics, 1977), 17.

52. *Survey of Experiences in School and Educational Plans: Version I,* conducted for United States Department of Education by Mathematical Policy Research, Inc. (Expiration Date: 31 August 1995), 1, 6, 8, 17, 18.

53. "Pennsylvania Guidelines and Application for the Drug-Free Schools and Community Act of 1986," Pennsylvania Department of Education (1992), 76-81.

54. Called the Exchange of Permanent Records Electronically for Students and Schools (SPEEDE/ExPRESS). Any education agency, local or national, can access the data. Data includes "student name, race, any involvement with a social service agency, health condition, and test scores."

55. *SCANS*, 61. A resumé for WORKLINK, "an electronic information system linking local schools and employers." It's now being used in several states. On page 64, *SCANS* says this resumé will begin in middle school and contain a record of portfolios, projects, etc.

56. Quoted from "Wellness and Me Portfolio Project for Lifetime Health," given to Lakeridge High students in 1993. This is the same school, in the opening of chapter 1, that used the "Values Appraisal Scale," which ask questions such as "I believe in a God who answers prayers."

57. Phone interview by author with Brenda White, 13 September 1994. White was informed by school official that the values appraisal would go into student's portfolio. Both in Oregon and North Caro-

lina parents succeeded in having the appraisal pulled. Are other schools around the country using it?

58. *SCANS*, 60. Promoted by the New Standards Project.

59. Memo from Pennsylvania Federation of Teachers, AFT, AFL-CIO Vice President Jack Steinberg to State Rep. Ron Gamble, 16 March 1993, 1.

60. John R. Criswell and Robert J. Zanotti, "Questions Teachers Ask about Literacy Portfolios: A Need for Rethinking before Answering," *Pennsylvania Educational Leadership* (Spring 1994): 23.

61. Nicholas D. Kristof, "Where Each Worker Is Yoked to a Personal File," *New York Times International*, 16 March 1992, A4.

62. Personal interview by author with Lan (last name withheld), 6 August 1994.

63. "Teachers Draw Inspiration, Perspiration at Summer Meeting," *The New Standard* (July 1994): 1.

64. "Rand Study Points To Problems in Vermont's Portfolio Assessment Program," *The Executive Educator* (February 1993): 6.

65. Michael Schrage, "Let's Get Computers out of the Classroom," *Los Angeles Times Syndicate*, May 1993.

66. Pete du Pont, "In Education, Outcome Is Input," *Providence Sunday Journal*, 24 April 1994, 1.

67. Ron Brandt, "On Outcome-Based Education: A Conversation with Bill Spady," *Educational Leadership* (December 1992/January 1993): 70.

68. *H.B. 1017: A Plain English Version*, 34, 35. (This cites H.B. 1017, Section 77, 101.)

69. Arthur M. Schlesinger, Jr., *The Disuniting of America: Reflections on a Multicultural Society* (New York: W. W. Norton & Company, 1991), 45.

70. Frank McNatt, "Citizens Deserve More Than Platitudes from Education Bureaucrats," *The Oregonian*, 14 April 1994.

71. "Connecticut's Common Core of Learning: Appendix B," Connecticut State Board of Education, 7 January 1987, 76.

72. *Model Learner Outcomes for International Education*, Department of Education, 1991, vii.

73. Ibid., 25.

74. Ibid., 12.

75. "Teaching Goals and Philosophy," Fifth Grade (1994–1995), one-page handout at parent's night.

76. "What Did You Do in School Today?" Channel 4 News, Oklahoma City, 1993.

77. *SCANS*, 81.

78. Adapted from Kentucky's Valued Outcomes, number 66. "Students demonstrate an understanding of, appreciation for, and sensitivity to a multicultural and world view."

79. Schlesinger, Jr., *Multicultural Society*, 71.

80. "Culture: A Shared Design for Living," *PSEA: The Voice For Education* (April 1993): 10, 11.

81. Written testimony by Dr. Scott Tyson, 1 June 1992. Given at a Pennsylvania State Board Of Education hearing on OBE in Monroeville, Pa.

82. Ibid.

83. Pat Buchanan, "We're No. 1," *Pittsburgh Post-Gazette*, 23 March 1994, B3.

84. Phone interview by author with Pat Hart, chairman of the Lake County School Board, 11 September 1994, and Pat Buchanan, "We're No. 1: Florida's Lake County School Board Has It Right," *Pittsburgh Post-Gazette*, 23 May 1994, B3.

85. Buchanan, "We're No. 1," B3.

86. Vincent Carroll, "Educators Who Deprecate Knowledge Have Lesson To Learn," *Rocky Mountain News*, 21 October 1993, 7A, and Vincent Carroll, "In Littleton, Colo., Voters Expel Education Faddists," *Wall Street Journal*, 18 November 1993, A20.

87. Daniel J. Singal, "The Other Crisis In American Education," *Atlantic Monthly* (November 1993): 62.

88. Art Spikol, "Who's In Charge?" *Writer's Digest* (October 1993): 64.

89. *The International Experience with School Leaving Examinations*, (Washington, D.C.: National Center on Education and the Economy, 1994), 4.

90. David Theis, "A Whole Lotta Learning Going On," *Effective School Practices* (Summer 1993): 17–23.

91. Open letter written by U. S. Congressman Dick Armey (Texas) to his colleagues in the Congress of the United States, "How Do You Spell Outcome-Based Education? G-O-A-L-S 2-0-0-0," 6 October 1993, 1.

92. Letter from Sen. Gilbert J. Dinello, 14 April 1993.

93. Adapted from Bettye Lewis's "ABC's of OBE," *Michigan Alliance of Families*, newsletter (July/August 1993). Used with permission.

94. D. Thomas King, "The Saturn School of Tomorrow: A Reality Today," *Technological Horizons in Education* (April 1992): 66–68.

95. Ibid.

96. *Minneapolis-St. Paul Tribune*, 14 May 1992, as quoted in a fact sheet from Pennsylvania State Representative Ron Gamble.

EIGHT

WILL THE REAL "SUCCESS" SCHOOL PLEASE STAND UP?

If all records told the same tale–then the lie passed into history and became truth.

—George Orwell, *1984*

OBE: Sounds Too Good to Be True

Success. Essential. Total Quality. A-Plus. World-class. Words sell. Those words, phrases—mnemonics—market outcome-based education, and people are buying.

High Success Network. Coalition of Essential Schools. Total Quality Classrooms. A-Plus Reform. World-class Education. You can almost hear the sound—success. Across America, these OBE models are becoming as familiar as loudly hyped American car prototypes. But, is it a Cadillac or an Edsel?

Imagine a car dealer telling you, "This car is *world-class. Quality* is written all over it. We're talking every *essential* feature." You'd think, "Sounds too good to be true." And, you would eagerly ask the obvious questions, "What about a warranty? This model has been road tested, hasn't it?" What if the dealer looked insulted, but he condescended to answer, "No warranty. As for road tests, the company did one or two; but no need to look at those results." Then, confidently he told you, "I know a lot about cars. Trust me." Would you buy that car for your children?

Kicking the Tires

That's what sociologists and educators are telling you about OBE. "Buy OBE. Although there's no guarantee, we'll show you a handful of successful pilot schools to prove it works. No need to look at them too closely. We know a lot more about education than you. Trust us."

Meanwhile, across the nation, concerned citizens are starting to kick OBE's tires, and those tires don't seem roadworthy. This is what some elected officials are finding:

> No research, studies, or pilot programs demonstrate the effectiveness or possible success of OBE. Quite to the contrary, OBE has been a disastrous failure.[1]
>
> —Pete du Pont,
> former governor of Delaware,
> policy chair of the National
> Center for Policy Analysis

> [OBE is a] disastrous educational experiment being forced on the most vulnerable, and yes, captive members of our society, our children.[2]
>
> —Randy Brandt,
> Arkansas representative

> Outcome-Based Education is being sold as something that it is not.[3]
>
> —Dan Boddicker,
> Iowa representative

> So far the record shows OBE has not been very successful when implemented.[4]
>
> —Gary Porter,
> North Dakota representative

> [OBE, called QPA in Kansas] involves "experimental/non-academic programs that lower academics."[5]
>
> —Darlene Cornfield,
> Kansas representative

> Contrary to the assertions made by supporters of OBE, there is no track record. . . . In fact, it has failed in most places where it has been tried.[6]
>
> —Mike Fisher, Pennsylvania senator

> This is too much money to be spending on experiments. . . . [OBE] may weaken educational standards for Virginia's children.[7]
>
> —L. Douglas Wilder, governor of Virginia

Virginia—OBE: DOA

Let's look at that last quote by a Virginia governor. It's from his landmark press release announcing that the Common Core of Learning [Virginia's OBE] was to be terminated. He explained that OBE was an expensive experiment ($6.7 million for one year[8]) that weakened academics. Reporting his decision, the *Richmond Times-Dispatch* said that on 15 September 1993, Governor Wilder "axed Outcome-Based Education." The newspaper's pithy title speaks volumes, "OBE: DOA."[9]

The *Washington Times* called it "Virginia's World Class Education Flop." This paper cynically observed, "Virginia's 'World Class' plan was something known as outcome-based education, a concept reassuring in name only."[10]

Why did this Democratic governor reverse his decision to push OBE reforms? According to the not-so-conservative *Washington Post*, he agreed with critics that outcome-based education would:

- restrict the power of local school boards
- emphasize teamwork, not the three Rs
- emphasize attitudes, not the three Rs

Actually, America's most powerful weapon—the pen (word processor)—first woke up Virginia's sleeping citizens. As usual OBE was slipping in quietly. But, a year-long series of the *Richmond Times-Dispatch's* probing editorials by staff writer Robert Holland set off a startling alarm.

Holland's articles, such as "Murder Merit: Pay the Price," which exposed OBE's disdain for competition; "Education Invades the Affective Domain," which described the reform's intended change of direction from academics into the psychological; "The Multicultural Express," "Labor Wants Electronic Pupil-Dossiers," and "School Restructuring, By Hillary" were read and reread.[11]

Virginians take pride in getting their children accepted into top colleges. So, Holland's articles grabbed not only their attention, but also their commitment to tell neighbors, to collar legislators, to educate superintendents, and to put Governor Wilder on notice.

In May 1993, Wilder's unanimously adopted restructuring blueprint was humming peacefully along. OBE's plan included integrated subjects, multicultural emphases, learner outcomes, assessments, de-emphasis of phonetics, fewer academics, more workforce skills, and—by 1996—compulsory attendance for all four-year olds. (Age four is targeted in OBE's 1984 federal grant proposal mentioned in chapter 1.) These were not ingredients well-educated parents wanted. Four months later, bowing to popular pressure, the governor declared OBE, "DOA." If parents hadn't kicked the tires, this wouldn't have happened.

FACT: *Less than a year earlier, Spady had identified Virginia as a national "pioneer" for OBE.*[12]

Cheri Took a Test Drive

Meet Cheri Yecke. She's thirty-something, brunette, and an anti-restructuring crusader. Cheri is also a 1991 finalist for the *Washington Post's* outstanding teacher award and Virginia's Stafford County teacher of the year. Her position to challenge restructuring is unique. Yecke's two daughters inadvertently became an OBE case study—rather like a before-and-after experiment.

From 1982 to 1984, both daughters attended schools in Minnesota's District 833. When the Yeckes moved to Virginia, the girls adapted well. After seven years, the family was transferred back to Minnesota, and they eagerly reenrolled both children in District 833. "We were in for a shock," says Yecke. During those seven years, the district implemented OBE. "Our daughters were academically 'light years' ahead of their peers."

Seventh grader Tiffany, who had always loved school, was begging to stay home. "The work was far too easy," says Yecke. "But worse, the other students ridiculed, in a cruel and demeaning way, any display of intelligence." Why? Students achieved status by non-performance. There were no deadlines. In this system, motivation was neither encouraged nor rewarded. Competition was discouraged. No one failed. Instead, they received *A*, *B*, or *I* (*Incomplete*). However, *I* didn't count in a student's grade point average, so why retake tests? By the end of the 1992 semester, in grades seven through twelve, more than 15,500 "Incompletes" were recorded—about half of all grades given.[13] During its nine years of OBE, District 833 Iowa Test of Basic Skills scores dropped significantly and steadily.[14]

After two years, the Yecke family moved back to Virginia. Ironically, Yecke was greeted by an all too familiar face—OBE. A face making boisterous claims of success. She had written articles exposing problems in Minnesota schools. Now, she saw that the frightening lies about OBE's "success-for-all" were spread on a national scale.

Was America experiencing a media blackout about OBE? If so, why? To get information, Yecki began calling, faxing, phoning, and networking around the country. Were other districts, other states, other nations rejecting OBE?

Other States Saying No

Iowa

"Now after several years of slow implementation our state is poised to encourage Outcome-Based Education statewide," wrote a discouraged Iowa state Representative Dan Boddicker, on 19 April 1993.[15] Realizing Iowa's outcomes "reek of political correctness," he wrote, "Our Department of Education has developed a list of goals and objectives [outcomes] ranging from 'Appreciation of Creativity' to 'Commitment to Lifelong Learning'. . . . There was no mention of academics in the stated goals and objectives."[16]

He faxed a letter of warning to his peers in Pennsylvania who, at that time, were also voting on OBE legislation. He summed up his grave misgivings about restructuring, "We must pray for our success [opposing OBE] because the future of our nation depends on our efforts."[17]

Grassroots Iowa groups shared the representative's zeal for stopping restructuring. One organization published *Iowa Report*, the nation's first anti-OBE newspaper. Some people fasted and prayed each Friday, calling their anti-OBE effort "Fabulous Fasting Fridays." Other organizations widely distributed "Stop Outcome-Based Ed" bumper stickers. Citizens got noisy. Legislators got angry and called outcomes, " 'politically correct, feel-good' goals."[18]

Loud objections and prayers paid off. In May 1993, the Department of Education released a surprising announcement. Headlines shouted, "Outcome Education Plan Altered: Statewide Education Goals Dropped."[19]

Alabama

Meanwhile, in the South, Kentucky folks warned Alabama citizens. A court ruling demanding equitable school funding would, no doubt, also tiptoe into Alabama—bringing with it an unexpected OBE package. What had begun as a "routine" financial lawsuit, resulted in Kentucky's *entire system* of elementary and secondary schools being declared unconstitutional. The court ordered state lawmakers to create a completely new system. That tactic forced through their outcome-based restructuring act (KERA).

Both states had hosted OBE promoter and Business Roundtable's senior advisor David Hornbeck (with his high consulting fee[20]). Alabamians knew that he applauded Kentucky's financial equity case to force OBE. In fact, he actually promotes using lawsuits to "provoke change."[21] Hornbeck offers the idea, "If we know how to achieve success with virtually all students, then there is a legal duty to do so."[22] Does he mean that—as an excuse to coerce unsuspecting lawmakers—states should create lawsuits over a separate issue, like the inequitable school tax problem? Then, would the court order legislators to come up with a "success-for-all" package (which someone waiting in the wings hands them, called outcome-based education)?

That's what Kansas did. As in Kentucky, a circuit court decision to equalize funding was used to declare all previous education legislation unconstitutional. To replace the old laws, a new "equitable" and "accountable" education bill had to be passed quickly. At midnight, someone offered a "success-for-all" education reform package, and Kansas representatives passed their outcome-based law (called QPA).

Accountability and *equity* were the buzz words. Missouri legislated its massive reform that identical way.[23] According to a computer bulletin board network called Prodigy, other states dealing with tax equity court orders included Maine, Vermont, Texas, Tennessee, Ohio, New Jersey, Arizona, and Massachusetts. Some coincidence, thought Alabamians.

Despite their laid-back Southern drawl, Alabamians know how to organize quickly. Citizens were ready in 1993 when a circuit judge ruled that public schools were not funded equitably. He issued a landmark court order to restructure the now "constitutionally deficient" public school system. His "remedy order" had OBE fingerprints all over it, including eliminating the Carnegie Units, the general track, and standardized tests; possible inclusion of the CIM, community service, and developing student learning goals [outcomes].[24]

People have been educated enough to know that "outcome-based education [called Alabama First] is a costly experimental fad that has failed in other states," said SCORE 100 spokesperson, Stephanie Bell. She plunked down a well-conceived, back-to-basics education reform plan. For the first time, an anti-OBE group was given enough warning to offer an alternative statewide plan. Were they successful? Initially.

Because the SCORE 100 members had time to educate the public, even Alabama's teachers' union wanted no part of OBE. Letters came to legislators from their peers in other states. Kentucky Rep. Thomas Kerr wrote, "I would urge Alabama legislators to use extreme caution. . . . I would recommend that your state steer clear of any proposal that uses components of outcome based education (OBE)."[25] In both regular and special legislative session, the state's $2 billion OBE plan was "killed."[26]

As this book goes to press, Bell, with her SCORE 100 group, hopes to implement a true success-for-all package—

it's a back-to-basics reform—so Alabama's children will be taught how to think, not what to think. (Citizens in another southern state, Mississippi, have adopted SCORE 100's name and ideas to fight their OBE-style reform act, which silently passed in 1994.)

Connecticut

"We're on the cutting edge here," bragged Connecticut's Board of Education chair Christina Burnham.[27] In 1994, Connecticut's OBE-style reform bill was scheduled to sail smoothly through the legislature.

Weren't prototypes of the new world-class education reform, like Old Saybrook's school system, already proving its success? Since 1987 to 1988, that district had spent more than fifty-nine thousand dollars[28] on converting into an OBE model, called Outcome Driven Developmental Model (ODDM—aptly pronounced "Oh, Dum").

Old Saybrook quietly embraced all the salient OBE features: abolishing standardized tests, exchanging phonics for "whole language," eliminating ability grouping, reducing homework, disparaging competition, embracing self-directed learning (children decide what they'll learn each day), introducing "problem solving" instead of mastering basic skills, and de-emphasizing textbooks. First grade basal readers and math textbooks had been put into locked closets.

One student, who had been in Old Saybrook's gifted/talented program, earned a near-failing 1.6 grade point average her freshman college year. Previous plans to major in engineering were gone forever. Another graduate—called "one of the brightest students ever to go through our school"—flunked his freshman courses at Brown.[29]

Connecticut's pending "reform" bill, with its $125 million price tag,[30] promised to put the entire state on the same "cutting edge" as Old Saybrook. That is, until several crusaders, with Ivy League backgrounds and briefcases stuffed with facts, barnstormed across the state. In their wake, anti-OBE chapters formed, calling themselves Committee to Save Our Schools (CT:SOS)—seventy of them.

An angry teachers' union joined the fight against the bill. One teacher explained that the school reform effort involved too few teachers and too many business people. (To promote this work force bill, business had lobbied hard and spent hundreds of thousands of dollars.[31])

Public opposition lacked money, but not determination. Every state legislator received lobby letters from the members of Committee to Save Our Schools stating that world-class education was irredeemably flawed, because it:[32]

- uses school children in educational experiments with a documented history of failure

- is an instant Budget Buster—it is outrageously expensive

- destroys local control (despite claims to the contrary)

- is part of a national movement driven by the federal government

- forces a new "politically correct" values-based curriculum

- sidesteps accountability for true academic results

Legislators heard the public outcry and read their criticisms. Frantically, bill proponents watered down legislation. Then, they changed its phraseology to read, "Results-Based Education" (instead of Outcome-Based). But, smoke 'n' mirror tricks didn't work. Before reaching the floor, the bill died. Connecticut's legislative defeat was astounding, especially since many other states had used its 1987 Common Core of Learning goals as a "success" model for their outcomes. Immediately, as in Alabama, the Constitution State's citizens began polishing a strong back-to-basics proposal before the next OBE legislative assault.

But, what was happening in local school districts? "The OBE movement is like a hydra-headed monster," warned CT:SOS leader Dr. Jeffrey Satinover. "You stamp it out at the state level, and it pops up at the local level."[33] He was alerting districts like Old Saybrook. However, one month after OBE's defeat at the state capitol, Old Saybrook's monster was beheaded. In plain English, a new superinten-dent and the school board threw it out—erasing another OBE "success" story.

Local "Successful" Districts—NOT!

Minnesota's Apple Valley-Rosemount-Eagan Schools, District 196

In 1991, when Apple Valley-Rosemount-Eagan schools (District 196) heard Minnesota was "evolving step by step into an outcome-based education state,"[34] they asked to guide those steps. As Minnesota's third largest district, citizens were eager to pilot OBE. They wanted to be its success story.

Instead, an academic nightmare began. "Our grades became 'A,' 'B' and 'I' for Incomplete—so no one could fail. One school handed out *ten thousand* 'Incompletes.' But did an 'I' in algebra mean a student couldn't begin geometry? It was a mess," remembers Christopher May, a member of Rosemount High Outcome-Based Education Review Task Force. He thumbs through a 150-page book filled with quotes from students, teachers, and parents. "Over 90 percent spoke against OBE. The harshest criticism came from students themselves."[35]

Eighth-grader Kirsten Hagen summed up her under-standing of its success-for-all theory: "OBE reminds me of a sign I saw in a restaurant once: 'If our food and service don't meet your expectations, then lower your expecta-tions.' "[36]

Recent graduate Steve Burdette added that "success" was created through OBE's grade inflation. "All we are doing with OBE is to call a C a B." Steve said that although he had a 3.0 grade point average, his class rank was only 350 out of 500. He vividly remembered having trouble in math class, yet passing a test on the seventh try. It wasn't because he bothered to study the material, but he says "the teacher decided she was sick of seeing my face."[37]

According to May, children retaking tests six and seven times bred sloppy study habits. Churning out new versions of the same exams exhausted teachers. As academics went down, parents' hostility went up. "Our task force found OBE does not work. Period."[38]

OBE failed because its assumptions about children were wrong. For instance, its success-for-all theory. Is OBE's idea to remove failure from schools academically sound? According to *District 196 Outcome-Based Education Review Task Force Report*, (which removed OBE), failure is normal, a natural part of the learning process. It can be turned into positive learning experiences. Therefore, the task force re-instituted the ranking of high schoolers academically. They also reestablished traditional grades of *A* through *F*. This report cancelled other OBE practices by stating:

- The primary purpose of public education is to teach academics.

- Positive self-esteem cannot be taught (but, it can be gained through the stretching and growth of current knowledge and skills).[39]

"By 1995 every piece of OBE is to be eradicated from our district," emphasizes May.

Statewide public outcry has shaken the Viking State's 1990 resolve "to become an outcome based education state."[40] However, beginning in 1996, Minnesota plans to eliminate the Carnegie Units—replacing them with outcomes.[41] How will schools meet outcomes without an outcome-based delivery system? What will happen to resistant districts such as Rosemount? Citizens must keep kicking OBE's tires.

Littleton, Colorado

Few districts in the country basked in more pro-OBE press coverage than Littleton, Colorado. This national OBE showcase was lauded as one of America's first districts to require outcomes, not "seat time" (English class, history class, etc.) to graduate. Slick publicity made the district look like it glowed with success. The fact that half of the staff had serious doubts about the program[42] was suppressed—until the 1993 school board election.

Many were determined to keep Littleton a national OBE success. Several months before the election, People for the American Way (PAW) opened an office nearby. They began suggesting that three back-to-basics candidates were all members of the "religious right"[43] (as if that were some plague). When someone leaked to the press that PAW's office space and phones had been donated by Colorado's teachers' union, an editor sarcastically commented, "The very people who are supposed to be teaching 'tolerance' are fully aware of the uses of bigotry."[44]

The editor added that Littleton's race was "slathered in sleaze." His newspaper had just received a letter accusing the back-to-basics candidates of belonging to the Flat Earth Society.[45] (In fact, one candidate holds a doctorate and wrote a physics textbook.) Then came the final blow: all voters received an open letter denouncing the three traditional candidates, signed by all fifteen principals.[46]

Throughout all these hardships, the three candidates tried to focus on the real issue, OBE. They never uttered a word about religious issues affecting schools. (None belonged to a denomination associated with the Religious Right—one didn't even attend any church. The three believed their religious affiliations were personal, not relevant to the campaign.) Instead, their topics centered on watered-down academics and the importance of factual knowledge. They asked why textbooks were being removed from classes and why students could fail all classes and still graduate if they passed Littleton's outcomes.

Colorado's aspens turned golden. It was November, and voters responded. They elected the back-to-basics slate by a nearly two-to-one margin. An article in the *Wall Street Journal* called it 1993's most significant education election in the nation.[47] The *Journal* continued, "Littleton proves that with the proper candidates, the movement toward a vague, 'skill-oriented' curriculum [OBE] can be stopped in its tracks."[48]

Checking *Facts*

But, nothing seemed able to stop OBE in the Keystone

State. In 1993, Pennsylvania became the first state to abolish the Carnegie Units and tie graduation requirements to outcomes.

In a nutshell, here's what happened: When discussion about state outcomes began, an anti-OBE firestorm erupted. In its heat, more than five hundred outcomes (which included phrases like "sexual orientation") were melted down to fifty-three,[49] which was still unacceptable. State legislators overwhelmingly defeated a statewide initiative which would force all districts to do performance-based education (OBE). Undaunted—and unelected—the Department of Education smugly mandated outcomes through the "back door," via a regulatory process.

But, state officials knew public opposition against OBE had run ten to one.[50] So, after OBE became law, the state had to calm angry citizens who were still crying, "Show us where it works. Will our children be OBE guinea pigs?"

"A Record of Success" section inside a *Facts* pamphlet from the Pennsylvania Department of Education was published to prove to doubting parents "that performance-based education works."[51] From the thousands of districts across our nation, it highlights four premiere OBE schools. Parents called those schools to verify *Facts'* facts. Listen to all four responses:

Red Bank, New Jersey: "We eliminated Mastery Learning seven years ago," said Dr. David Squires, head of curriculum. "Red Bank schools are not under any OBE banner."[52]

Dodge City, Kansas: "I certainly would *not* put us in the 'success' category," said Dr. Colvin, high school principal. "We're only in the beginnings of OBE. Some people like it, others hate it. Tell your Department of Education to take us off their success list!"[53]

Johnson City, New York: (This district developed the ODDM, Outcomes-Driven Developmental Model—see "Old Saybrook" section.) The assistant principal resisted a request from the telephone interviewer for SAT scores. One set of scores he released for 1992 through 1993 averaged 957 total—not very impressive for *the* "model" district in the nation, after twenty-three years of using an outcome-based program. Of the eleven districts surrounding Johnson City, not one has been impressed enough to adopt ODDM.[54]

Bay City, Michigan: "Take us off your state's 'success' list," said David Johnson, counselor at Bay City Public School. "We were an OBE school—all the ODDM gurus were here [they used the OBE model from Johnson City]. We tried it for three years. Then we threw it out six years ago. Spent millions to bring it into the schools. Slush funds were depleted. I can't say this strongly enough: OBE is a true swear word in our district!"[55]

Pennsylvania parents are still demanding, "Show us where it works."

Will the Real Successful School Please Stand Up?

America's schools need help. If OBE doesn't work, what does? Remember the television show "What's My Line?" It might make reform a lot simpler if we could ask, "Will the Real Successful School Please Stand Up?" In that situation, OBE emissaries (wearing their huge success-for-all lapel buttons) would shuffle, stretch, and smile confidently at the camera. But, you would hear the hushed audience gasp when an unlikely delegate slowly rose from her seat.

Gertrude Williams: A Giant

When Barclay School principal Gertrude Williams stands, everyone notices. Although Williams weighs only eighty-five pounds, she has the backbone of a giant.

She had a dream—no, it was a vision. She could see her Barclay school, in crime-infested Baltimore, transformed academically to look like Baltimore's private academy, Calvert School. But, how could that ever happen? At Barclay, students were tossed endlessly about by the latest teaching fads the bureaucrats drummed up. Meanwhile, students at Calvert mastered the three Rs in a solid curriculum, smoothly polished over the years.

Williams was convinced that her students needed a disciplined, traditional education like that required at Calvert.

So, in 1988, she developed a proposal showing how to use the Calvert curriculum at her school. Unfortunately, her enthusiasm hit a wall of resistance. Her ideas weren't "progressive." Baltimore's school superintendent rejected the plan as a "rich man's curriculum" unusable in Williams' mostly impoverished school.

For two years Williams continued to ask, "How can a child learn if the curriculum is always changing? We need to try some proven strategies."[56] Finally, in 1990, the Calvert/ Barclay project was born.

Traditional Education vs. OBE

Three short years later, when compared with other students in model schools, Barclay pupils scored at or near the top in spelling, punctuation, grammar, and verbal expression. Soaring scores have attracted a waiting list from other school districts.[57]

"Educators come from all over the U.S. as well as countries like Australia and Japan to observe us," says Williams in her raspy, but gentle voice. "Why? Our curriculum has a strong academic base in phonics, grammar, history. I'm not for any gimmick—like outcome-based education."

"Outcome-based education doesn't educate children; it trains them," she explains. "That's because OBE was developed by industry. Not educators. So industry decides what students should know and be able to do, without properly teaching basics. That does not prepare youngsters for life."

"For example, think about Florida's recent devastating hurricane." Always an educator, Williams often explains by examples. "Some houses were plain and inexpensive. But if solidly built with a basement, they stood. Fancy homes costing lots of money—without basements—blew away. Children need a foundation of basic skills. Then, as adults they're prepared to weather career storms. They'll find new jobs. OBE doesn't give you enough basic skills to regroup."[58]

Stand Up for Success

Stressing basics has made Barclay's education truly transformational. It changes lives. In kindergarten, Dorothy Dallas was non-verbal. She'd cry when asked to print her name. Now, in fifth grade, she writes and spells beautifully, well above grade level.

Although Justin Yorkman was marked as being "at risk" for dropping out of school, by fourth grade he was working at a sixth grade level. When Justin's family moved, he chose to endure a forty-five minute bus ride to attend Barclay.

"It's not the children who should be labeled 'at risk'; it's progressive curriculums," says Williams.

About fifty years ago, a teacher told a shy seventh grader named Gertude Williams, "You must always stand up for yourself in life." Today, Williams stands tall; not for herself, but for successful education.

Endnotes

1. Pete du Pont, "In Education, Outcome Is Input," *Providence Sunday Journal*, 4 April 1994.

2. Letter from Arkansas Rep. Randy Brandt, 13 April 1993.

3. Letter from Iowa Rep. Dan Boddicker, 19 April 1993.

4. Letter from North Dakota Rep. Gary Porter, 12 April 1993.

5. Letter from Kansas Rep. Darlene Cornfield, 8 July 1993.

6. Letter from Pennsylvania Sen. Mike Fisher, 15 July 1993.

7. Press statement issued by Virginia Governor Wilder, "Governor Wilder Calls for Immediate Disbandment of Common Core of Learning Programs and Experiments," Advisory to the Media, 15 September 1993, 2.

8. Ibid.

9. Op/Ed., "OBE:DOA," *Richmond Times-Dispatch*, 16 September 1993, A14.

10. Editorial, "Virginia's World-Class Education Flop," *Washington Times*, 17 September 1993, A22.

11. Available in a packet, "Outcome-Based Education: The Outcome in Virginia, The Nationwide Controversy," *Richmond Times-Dispatch*.

12. Ron Brandt, "On Outcome-Based Education: A Conversation with Bill Spady," *Educational Leadership* (December 1992/January 1993): 68, 70.

13. Phone interview by author with Cheri Pierson Yecke, 21 September 1994, and three articles by Cheri Pierson Yecke, "Outcome-Based Education: Is It Working?" *Bulletin Publishing* (13 February 1992): A12, and "OBE: The Work Ethic and Achievement," *Bulletin Publishing* (27 February 1992), and "Beware: Va. Education Reform May Rise From The Dead" *Stafford County Sun*, 20, 21 October 1993.

14. "Iowa Test of Basic Skills" District 833 (Composite Scores), grades 3–8, 1982 to 1992.

15. Letter, Boddicker, 19 April 1993.

16. Ibid.

17. Ibid.

18. Mark Siebert, "Statewide Education Goals Dropped," *Register*, 7 May 1993, A1.

19. Ibid.

20. Stephanie Bell, "School Tax Backers Should Listen To Opposition," *Montgomery Advertiser*, 10 July 1994, D1. Hornbeck received fifty thousand dollars from Montgomery, Alabama alone—three hundred per day from the state.

21. Hornbeck and Lester M. Salamon, *Human Capital and America's Future* (Baltimore, Johns Hopkins University Press: 1991), 365.

22. Ibid., 367.

23. In 1993, Missouri legislated SB 380 to restructure education around performance standards after a state circuit court judge ruled Missouri's education funding was not "equitable."

24. Proposed "Remedy Order" from the circuit court of Montgomery County, Alabama, 28 September 1993, 1-73.

25. Letter from Kentucky Rep. Thomas R. Kerr, 7 October 1993.

26. John Peck, "Reform Foes Point To Tax Rejection," *Huntsville Times*, 30 June 1994, B1.

27. Kenneth Von Kohorn, "Educational Experiments Can Damage Our Children," *Greenwich Time*, 9 February 1994, A15.

28. Alix Biel, "Superintendent Recommends Dropping Outcome-Based Education," *Hartford Courant*, 8 June 1994.

29. Von Kohorn, "Educational Experiments," A15.

30. Susan Faber, "Education Reform Adrift As Factions Take Positions," *Town Times*, 5 May 1994, 1.

31. Robert A. Frahm, "'Watered-Down' School Reform Bill Likely To Fail," *Hartford Courant*, 28 April 1994, 1.

32. Letter to Connecticut legislators from Committee to Save Our Schools, 10 March 1994.

33. Jim Blakely, "OBE Opponents Go on the Attack," *Minutem News*, 12 May 1994, 1.

34. *A Minnesota Vision for OBE*, Minnesota Department of Education Division of Instructional Practices, February 1990, 1.

35. Phone interview by author with Christopher May, 25 September 1994. Copies of this book *Comments about Outcome-Based Education* are available from School District 196.

36. Debra O'Connor, "Students Tell Why They Dislike New OBE Teaching Method," *St. Paul Pioneer Press*, 9 February 94.

37. O'Connor, "Students Tell Why": n.p.

38. Phone interview by author with Christopher May, 25 September 1994.

39. *District 196 Outcome-Based Education Review Task Force Interim Report*, Independent School District 196, 8 April 1994, 5, 6, 7, 8.

40. In 1992, the Minnesota Board of Education responded to testimonies at 23 meetings regarding the "Outcome-Based Graduation Requirements." As a result, the DOE altered its OBE requirements from "Outcome Based Graduation Standards" to "Results Oriented Graduation Rule."

41. Mary Jane Smetanka, "Students Will Be Forced To Work For Outcomes, Not Diplomas," *Star Tribune*, 12 September 1993, A19.

42. Greg Griffin, "Some Applaud Direction 2000, Others Critical," *Littleton Independent*, 7 January 1993, 15.

43. David Shiflett, "Littleton School Board Race Becomes Slathered In Sleaze," *Rocky Mountain News*, 16 October 1993.

44. Ibid.

45. Ibid.

46. Vincent Carroll, "In Littleton, Colo., Voters Expel Education Faddists," *Wall Street Journal*, 18 November 1993, A20.

47. Ibid.

48. Ibid.

49. Michael deCourcy Hinds, "Where School Is More Than Just Showing Up," *New York Times*, 21 July 1994, B10.

50. Memo from Mary M. Dupuis, president of the Pennsylvania Association of Colleges and Teacher Educators (PAC-TE) to PAC-TE members, 2 February 1993, 1 (a group promoting OBE).

51. "A Record Of Success," *Facts About Pennsylvania's Education Reform*, Commonwealth of Pennsylvania.

52. Phone interview by author with Dr. David Squires, 28 February 94, and phone interview by author, 21 September 1994.

53. Phone interview by author with Dr. Colvin, 14 February 94, and phone interview by author with Dr. Colvin, 21 September 1994.

54. Phone interview by John Spillane with Assistant Principal Alan, 14 February 94.

55. Phone interview by John Spillane with Dave Johnson, 14 February 94, and phone interview by author with Dave Johnson, 22 September 1994.

56. Lavinia Edmunds, "The Woman Who Battled the Bureaucrats," *Reader's Digest* (December 1993): 145.

57. Ibid.

58. Phone interview by author with Gertrude Williams, 29 September 1994.

NINE

WHAT'S A PERSON TO DO?

Sometimes, too, they talked of engaging in active rebellion against the Party, but with no notion of how to take the first step.

—George Orwell, *1984*

Voices from the Battlefront

War is raging in the classroom. It's a battle between Outcome-Based Education (OBE) and traditional education (three Rs). Is using an analogy of "war" a little strong? Maybe OBE is just a fad, like "new math" or language labs. After all, education bureaucrats constantly dish up new teaching approaches to justify their think-tank jobs.

If you doubt that this is a war, talk to Bev Bennett. She's a Nebraska mother who always trusted the public schools. But, Bev had worked for a Nebraska state senator and researched OBE. When she found it stressed behavioral objectives rather than academics, she formed a Nebraska group and began speaking out against OBE in her state. In April 1993, while attending a three-day state education conference, she noticed that two men seemed to be following her.

By the third day, she was getting angry. So, with a small, black tape recorder in hand, Bev turned and confronted the men, "Why are you following me? Who authorized this?" She recorded their reply. Yes, they admitted, they were observing her. The men told Bev they were under-

cover police officers ordered by the governor's office to follow her. Bev was furious and immediately filed a complaint with the Nebraska attorney general's office.[1]

Soon afterward, the *Lincoln Journal Star* reported that Nebraska's teachers' union raised dues by four dollars to "combat . . . the darkest threat in the history of public education."[2] Evidently, government officials considered Bev, armed with her files of OBE research, a "dark threat."

Meanwhile, in another state, Pennsylvania's teachers' union commissioned a Taxpayer's New Right Task Force (TNT). Its regional offices are peppered throughout the state to "study and provide information to Pennsylvania State Education Association [PSEA] members as to the composition, membership, and activities of far right wing groups as they affect education and our Association."[3] According to their flier, the TNT (sounds like dynamite, doesn't it?) will also "help in stopping such groups from forming."[4] How will this watchdog task force go into communities to stop parents from forming organizations against OBE? Kathy Riggle found out. Kathy is a young mother who formed a group in the Lake Erie region to oppose OBE. On a public school bulletin board, the northwest regional TNT posted Kathy's name, as well as the name of her church.[5]

Marsha Hulshart calls what's going on in her school a war. Her husband is a school board member in Pennsylvania's Daniel Boone district, which has used outcome-based education since 1988. Marsha says that teachers not fully implementing OBE in their classrooms, or who speak out against it openly, are labeled "toxic."[6]

Why are bureaucrats trying so hard to silence ordinary folks? This is a "no holds barred," "take no prisoners" war. Kathy, Marsha, and Bev will tell you OBE is one fad that won't go away unless many other citizens roll up their sleeves and volunteer to fight. It's a battle over who will control America's children.

Get Smart

At this point, you may be saying, "I'm willing to join the

battle. But, what's a person to do?" First, you've already shown you care by wading through a book like ours. Having a desire to help is the first hurdle.

Now, get as smart about OBE as you can. Educate yourself. Without realizing it, you've already gotten a jump-start by reading this book. However, videos, audio cassettes, articles, and other books are also available.[7] Read materials from both those opposing OBE and its advocates. Often what promoters of OBE write is more outrageous than anything we critics are saying. (For example, the High Success Network will send you articles by Dr. Spady, free.[8]) Don't feel overwhelmed by the complexity of OBE; this restructuring of education is complicated. It takes time to understand. Most of us have to re-read books and re-watch videos. Highlight what you learn and pass it on to friends.

"Divide and conquer" is a helpful maxim while studying outcome-based education. After you have acquired a general overview of OBE/restructuring, you may want to choose a few areas to learn about in depth, such as strategic planning, GOALS 2000, extended-time class blocks, etc. You might ask a friend to master early childhood education, the certificates of mastery, or self-directed learning. Then, swap information. Think about writing summaries or making an audio cassette to inform others.

Keep in mind, OBE is an experiment. Getting information about districts that have thrown it out after a few years is most helpful. Also, if schools near you are using OBE (or some other outcome-based model), request a comparison of their national test scores over several years. Also, gather facts from the media about OBE's failure. For example, *U.S. News & World Report* revealed that the OBE-like experiment which began in 1988, with the Rochester, New York thirty-two thousand student school system, wasn't doing well. Although it was hailed as "a restructuring laboratory for the state and nation,"[9] recent results show problems. In 1987, 23 percent of Rochester's pupils earned New York State Regents Diplomas (the most rigorous diploma granted). Four years later, only 18 percent qualified. By 1991, 70 percent of the freshmen of Wilson Magnet School (Rochester's finest school) flunked the state's basic math test.[10]

You may be thinking, "So much information to gather. So much to do." Don't get discouraged by the scope of OBE/restructuring. It's a temptation we all have. This will be a long race, so concentrate on jumping one hurdle at a time. You've already come out of the starting block; you're over the first hurdle, and running.

How Do I Protect My Children?

Before you run too far, a word of advice. Most of us in this battle try to hold fast to three principles: God first, family second, and the OBE fight third. Unless you keep that priority, the battle for children will be lost on the home front.

After you've educated yourself, what should you do? Start at home with your own children. Be a nosy parent. Look at all their books and papers and ask lots of questions.

Don't just inquire how school went that day; instead use conversation openers like, "Did you see any movies? Did your class have any visitors? What did you talk about in history, English, science, or health today?" When you notice something in a textbook or on a test which raises questions, or when your child says something that you don't feel comfortable with, sit down immediately and talk about it.

Your time and your words are excellent tools to help your child see through the manipulation of OBE. No matter how busy you are, fulfill your responsibility to instill your belief system in your youngsters. Take time to teach them your family's ethics. Do not relinquish your parental duty to a government school.

For instance, as we've seen in previous chapters, "honesty" is one of the *SCANS* skills, therefore it's an outcome in many states. Will a government school define honesty as you would at home? In one OBE junior high class studying decision-making, a unit is called "How do *You* Spell Honesty?" Honesty is summed up, "It's sometimes very hard to decide what's right and what's wrong. Rather than black and white decisions, we'll have to deal with shades of gray."[11] In other words, honesty is defined in shades of gray. Don't you want your children to believe cheating on a test is wrong? Many decisions, such as sexual fidelity within marriage, are based on black and white—not on "shades of gray."

Share your faith and family traditions with your children. Tell them about the importance of competition in a capitalistic system. Discuss our nation's heritage and how vital the spirit of individualism is to maintaining freedom. Most important, study your book of worship together and then explain why certain beliefs must never be compromised. Warn children that what they are taught in school may conflict with many family values.

Protection of Pupil Rights

Draw lines of protection around your children at school. Any program that receives federal funds is governed by the Protection of Pupil Rights amendment to GOALS 2000. It requires any school district giving a survey, examination, or questionnaire that asks your child about such things as 1) attitudes, 2) beliefs, 3) family relationships, 4) family income, 5) sexual behavior, to inform parents that this right to privacy exists. Where you live, try to get a state version of this pupil rights act legislated to protect students' privacy in state-financed programs.

Although some school districts are not very receptive, you have the authority to look at anything your child sees (surveys, videos, plays, tests), as well as all school records.

You're the Only One

One mother asked a secretary for copies of all the textbooks her kindergartner would be using. The secretary told her that she didn't think parents were allowed to see them. The mother insisted and ended up talking to the principal:

> He said, "You're the only parent who has ever asked
> to see these."

She said, "So?"

"Well, what are you looking for—what do you expect to find?"

She said, "When I first asked, nothing. But the longer this conversation goes on, the more I'm beginning to wonder."

The mother got the books. She avoided two major pitfalls that parents stumble into. First, she ignored the statement that she was the only one. Your rights as a parent do not depend on how many other parents get involved. Second, she challenged the statement that implied that she was on a witch hunt because she asked to see materials. No parent has to justify a request for information. Parents are entitled to information. It makes no difference whether you're alarmed or simply curious.

Put It in Writing

One mother, who went to the district for information and was denied access to it, took a sheet of paper out of her purse and wrote: "On [date], I [her name] requested [name of material] from [district official's name] and was denied access." Then, she signed her name and handed the paper to the official, asking him to sign it. The official refused. So, the mother turned to her companion and asked her to sign that she had witnessed the incident. Suddenly, the material became available. Her secret? She was persistent and focused and immediately created a written record of the official's behavior.

Make Children and Parents "OBE Smart"

Teach your children to recognize intrusive questions and how they can avoid answering them. For example, when journals are required, you can try the technique used by an Indiana parent. She instructed her children to write the date and follow that heading with a report on the day's weather.

Questionnaires do not have to be answered by parents or children. In one Pennsylvania school district, a parents' questionnaire on reading began by asking how well their children behaved at home. Most mothers and fathers felt uncomfortable disclosing private information about how their youngsters acted, but answered the question anyway. However, one father refused to fill out the questionnaire. When he asked other mothers and dads, "Why should we fill it out?" other parents also began erasing their answers. He made his concerns public, raising awareness in other parents, and the questionnaire was discontinued in that district.

How to Stand Up Publicly

When you must go public with objections, you should remember a few guidelines:

1. Be factual. Don't exaggerate the incident. Otherwise, you will be dismissed as hysterical.

2. Personalize your presentation. Use examples from the curriculum, worksheets, or classroom experience.

3. Offer positive alternatives.

4. Stay focused. Don't get sidetracked and start discussing past incidents, personal reasons for not liking OBE, or why the football team is losing.

5. Stay calm. Angry people can be manipulated, so learn to smile. In one public meeting on a proposed AIDS education program, a mother questioned the accuracy of the AIDS information. Immediately, she was told to come forward, stand in the front of the center aisle of the auditorium, and repeat her question. She quietly walked down the long aisle to the front of the crowded room. The presenter then pointed at her and said, "Well, you can keep your children in a glass bubble if you want, if you're that afraid." The audience froze. But, the mother smiled and said, "If I am in error, tell me exactly what I've said that isn't accurate. But if I'm correct, how does ridiculing me protect my children?"

The meeting was abruptly dismissed. The AIDS program was scrapped. Why? Because the mother stayed calm and focused on her specific objection.

6. Present a specific course of action. Work to have

districts adopt policies that protect privacy rights (required now by all federal programs). Privacy rights should ensure that validated research be available in support of any educational program adopted by the district; experimental programs be conducted on a voluntary basis; and, available information in the district clearly states parental rights to opt out of objectionable programs.

The first time you speak against OBE publicly will seem like jumping a high hurdle. You'll be nervous. Just know your facts well. Document your sources and personalize your presentation. Remember, it makes no difference whether you have a Ph.D. from Harvard or haven't finished high school. As a parent, as a taxpayer, your qualifications couldn't look more impressive.

How to Grab Legislators' Lapels

Pen Power

As you saw in previous chapters, much of what is happening in our schools is being driven by state and federal legislation. But, previously passed OBE/restructuring acts can be repealed. New legislation can be stopped. Although it sounds overwhelming, it's as simple as the "lapel effect."

If something bothers you, you can contact your local representatives and (figuratively) grab them by the lapels. That gets their attention. How do you "grab lapels"? Get to know your elected officials. Write to them on issues that concern you. Here's how:

- Keep your letters brief.
- Address only one issue.
- Say what you want them to do, specifically.
- Ask for a reply, not a form letter.
- Be persistent.

Persistence pays off. One father wrote to his representative on an education issue:

Dear Representative ——,

I am in favor of [the bill number] because I believe

that it protects parental rights. I am asking you to co-sponsor and vote for this bill. Please tell me what you intend to do.

Sincerely,

———

That dad got a response:

Dear Mr. ———,

Thank you for your letter about [bill number]. I will keep your opinion in mind when I act on this important issue.

Sincerely,

———

The father was not satisfied with the response, so he wrote again.

Dear Representative ———,

Thank you for your prompt response. Unfortunately, you didn't say anything. I am asking you to co-sponsor and vote for [bill number]. Please let me know what you intend to do.

Sincerely,

———

The representative responded again.

Dear Mr. ———,

Thank you for your letter about [bill number]. I support the concept of the bill.

Sincerely,

———

The father decided to try one more time.

Dear Representative ———,

I am happy to hear that you support the concept of [bill number]. I would be even happier if you would co-sponsor and vote for the bill. Please tell me how you will act in this particular matter.

Sincerely,

———

Finally, the representative wrote:

Dear Mr. ———,

I will co-sponsor and vote for the passage of the bill.

Sincerely,

———

And he did, because his constituent was persistent.

In dealing with elected officials, don't forget to thank them for their favorable votes. People remember a kind word for a long time.

Try to give them information in small digestible bites. They don't have time to read long documents, so prepare brief, accurate summary statements that they can quickly scan.

Up Close and Personal

Also, meet with your local legislators at their home offices. To call for an appointment, you'll find legislators' numbers and addresses listed in the middle of the phone book (often on blue pages). Organize what you'll say before going. Bring classroom examples of how OBE is affecting your school. Show them outcomes and bills from other states. Let them know it is failing in many schools. Most legislators believe OBE is unique to their state.

Reach large numbers of representatives through a legislative breakfast or a working lunch at your state capitol. How? By asking a "friendly" legislator to send invitations and reserve a room for you. Meanwhile, arrange a formal twenty minute presentation followed by a period for questions. Distribute a one or two-page handout with newsclips or examples of papers from the classroom.

Rally Round the Rotunda

In 1994, citizens of Kentucky and Alabama joined forces. They gathered at Kentucky's state capitol to protest OBE/ restructuring. Because they sent a news release to the media, the protest was featured in a leading education newspaper, *Education Week* (9 February 1994). Similarly, other grassroots groups successfully organized anti-OBE "rally round the rotunda" events. How is this done? First, get legislators from each House to sponsor the rally. Next, notify the press. A few days before your state gathering, prepare "fact packs" (folders stuffed with several examples of how OBE affects the classroom, some newsclips showing where OBE has failed, and a one or two-page fact sheet about OBE). Be sure to have extra "fact packs" to share with the press during the rally. Make enough so that, immediately after the meetings, packets of information about OBE can be hand-delivered to each legislator's office.

Elections

Become involved in elections and politics at every level. You, as one person, can make a difference. An elected official out West gives this example:

Out of one hundred people, only fifty will be registered. Of the fifty, only half will be in a particular party. Of that twenty-five, only sixty percent will vote. Of that, about one-third will get involved in working for a candidate. So, five people out of every one hundred can dramatically affect an election.

Be one of those five people. Much of what is happening can only be turned around with legislation. And, if legislators in your area know that you are willing to work for those whom you support, they are more likely to listen to you.

Also, you can run for school board or help elect school board members whose reform platform is founded on back-to-basics education, rather than an experimental model such as OBE. Or, volunteer for your strategic planning committee. In Pennsylvania, fifty-three outcomes are mandated. Although schools can't delete any of these, each school may write additional outcomes. One member of a strategic planning committee in a Pennsylvania school district effectively neutralized the intent of OBE by adding these outcomes:

Pa. Student Learning Outcome: All students evaluate advantages, disadvantages, and ethical implications associated with the impact of science and technology on current and future life.

Added Outcome: Whenever an ethical judgment is called for, the ethical standard used should be identified; and the Western Judeo/Christian ethic should be normative.

Pa. Student Learning Outcome: All students evaluate the implications of finite natural resources and the need for conservation, sustainable agricultural development, and stewardship of the environment.

Added Outcome: "Finite" resources and "conservation" schools of thought represent only one view of how environmental problems should be solved. Competing views should also be considered.

Pa. Student Learning Outcome: All students demonstrate an understanding of the history and nature of prejudice and relate their knowledge to current issues facing communities, the United States, and other nations.

Added Outcome: Prejudice referred to is prejudice against others on the basis of race, color, national origin, religion, age or the fact that they are male or female. The District does not regard moral or religious opposition to, for example, homosexuality, pedophilia, and incest, as prejudice.

Pa. Student Learning Outcome: All students demonstrate that they can work effectively with others.

Added Outcome: Students will also learn that not all matters are negotiable and that moral convictions sometimes require that individuals must refuse to cooperate with others.

*Cooperative learning/collaborative learning teams in which students receive grades based upon how other team members perform should ordinarily **not** be used—recognizing that the public school classroom contains students with widely varying intelligence, experience and motivations—and is **not** parallel to the business workplace. Workplace teams are constituted because of each team member's particular skills. Monitored checking devices prevent individual irresponsibility.*

Pa. Student Learning Outcome: All students use effective research and information management skills, including locating primary and secondary sources of information with traditional and emerging library technologies.

Added Outcome: These skills should ordinarily be developed by requiring students to write actual essays, papers, and compositions and by doing research in substantive courses. Skills should not be divorced from content.

Pa. Student Learning Outcome: All students read and use a variety of methods to make sense of various kinds of complex texts.

Added Outcome: All students should be competent in the rules of phonics as part of learning to read.

How to Educate Others about OBE

Hear Ye! Hear Ye!—Town Meetings

Except for baseball and apple pie, nothing is more American than the town meeting. We mentioned how effective this was in such states as Connecticut, where—in a matter of months—seventy anti-OBE groups were formed.

Schedule a town meeting in any public place, such as a church, a Lion's Club, library, or school. To find out if your school permits outside organizations to use its facilities 1) contact the district's central office; 2) identify yourself with a group (if you are only a few loosely organized citizens, you can say something like, "Parents Involved in Education" or "Concerned Taxpayers"); and 3) request space as well as any necessary equipment, such as VCR, overhead projector, or microphone.

Advertise several weeks in advance. Use radio spots, church bulletins, supermarket bulletin boards, fliers stuffed in mailboxes. At the meeting, hand out condensed information about OBE, with an article or two about its philosophy and failures. Make available a sign-up sheet for those who want to join your group.

Town meetings can either feature one presenter or several speakers representing both sides. Invite school officials and legislators. With permission from the speakers, capture the event with a video camera and audio cassette recorders. Use copies of the tapes to inform others about OBE.

Newsletters

Write a newsletter. It's as easy as tickling the keys on a typewriter or word processor. If you need more information in order to write about OBE, you might look up endnote sources in this book. Go to your local library, get copies of the articles, and send them out with a summary. Use anecdotes and updates from other newsletters you receive. A computer bulletin board service, such as Prodigy, is an excellent tool to keep abreast of what's going on with OBE in different states.

After harvesting facts to summarize, you might also explain to readers the problems associated with OBE practices such as multiage classes, elongated class periods, school-based clinics, revised report cards, the elimination of honors courses, the Certificate of Initial Mastery. Local legislators' offices can get you copies of education bills so you can tell readers about pending OBE-reform legislation.

For duplicating your newsletter, twenty-four hour copy centers usually have reasonable rates. If your group incorporates as a not-for-profit organization, you can save money using a bulk rate permit. Asking subscribers for a modest donation will help defray expenses.

Coffee Klatsches

Many groups get started with informal home gatherings. You can watch a video or listen to an audio tape. Or, you might bring a speaker to tell the group about OBE.

Getting More Information

To obtain a copy of your state's outcomes, call or write your state Department of Education or governor's office. Because various states/districts are changing terminology and calling outcomes "performance standards," "learner outcomes," "quality standards," "results standards," you may have to use one of those names when asking if your state has completed its list of outcomes.

Also, ask if an education reform act has been passed within the past four years. If so, request a copy.

Let's Network

Fighting OBE can make you feel lonelier than the Maytag repairman. Organizations are available to help you network, both at state and national levels. To get OBE information or to find contacts in your state, call: Concerned Women for America (800) 458-8797, Eagle Forum (314) 721-1213, National Parents Commission (814) 539-3165, or Public Education Network (412-452-5708).

Also, you can network through computer bulletin boards. It's crucial to have a national perspective so you can see what legislation is headed toward your state, and how classrooms are being affected. Networking helps you learn how others are dealing with problems similar to ones you're facing in your school district.

What's a Person to Do?

Outcome-based education is not another education fad. It will not just go away. Our schools are fast becoming human resource factories. Can they again become centers of academic learning? Only if we are willing to fight for them.

But, the army opposing OBE is small. Much battleground has been lost already, simply because most citizens are still unaware a war is raging. They are sleeping through a battle for the souls of America's children.

However, there is still time. We can stop this assault on our children's values. But only if *every* parent, *every* grandparent, *every* citizen acts *now*.

Endnotes

1. Phone interview by author with Bev Bennett, 16 June 1994. Bev added: "I let the undercover officer know that I was taping his response, and he acknowledged that he was following me. In the course of the event, I talked to four individuals and all confirmed that there were undercover police officers at the Nebraska Department of Education Staff Development Conference in April 1993. I talked to the Nebraska Center for Continuing Education Conference director, and he told me that an individual from the governor's office had authorized the surveillance."

2. Jack Kennedy, "NSEA Raises Dues To Combat New Right," *Lincoln Journal-Star*, 25 April 1993.

3. TNT Taxpayers New Right Task Force, Pennsylvania State Education Association.

4. Ibid.

5. Taxpayers New Right Task Force, Northwestern Region PSEA, 5 January 1993.

6. Marsha Hulshart, "Beware Of OBE's Hidden Cost," *West Chester Daily Local News*, 23 February 1993.

7. An excellent packet of OBE articles, "Outcome-Based Education: The Outcome In Virginia," written by Robert Holland, is available through Family Research Council, (800) 225-4008.

8. The High Success Network, Inc., P.O. Box 1630, Eagle, Colorado, 81631. (800)-642-1979. See titles of Dr. Spady's articles mentioned in previous endnotes.

9. Robert Holland, "Rochester Is the Model, and Results Are Dismal," *Richmond Times-Dispatch*, 28 July 1993.

10. Thomas Toch and Jerry Buckley, "The Blackboard Jumble," *U.S. News & World Report* (25 May 1992): 33.

11. *The Curriculum Guide For Family Life Sciences : A Co-Educational Activity Approach To Learning*, The Junior High School, Mt. Lebanon School District, Pittsburgh, Pennsylvania, 1991, 136.

GLOSSARY

The purpose of Newspeak was not only to provide a medium of expression for the world-view and mental habits... but to make all other modes of thought impossible.

—George Orwell, *1984*

ASSESSMENT. A test that measures what a student has mastered. Assessments differ from traditional tests by de-emphasizing facts and content-centered material of a discipline. Assessments may require students to demonstrate skills, attitudes or behaviors, such as acceptance of beliefs of others and lack of prejudice.

> **Alternative assessment.** Allows a student to substitute tasks to show proficiency in a particular area (e.g., a student who cannot do the math algorithm may use a calculator).

> **Authentic assessment.** Involves a student's ability to perform outcomes in a "real-world" setting (e.g., building a bridge with paper clips rather than taking an exam; pasting pictures in a book rather than memorizing passages).

> **Criterion-referenced.** Score is based solely on a comparison of a particular student's performance to a pre-set standard (e.g., 6 X 6 = 36), so every student could fail or pass an assessment.

> **Group assessment.** Involves performing in a group setting, with students interacting to accomplish a task and receiving a group grade regardless of individual performance within the group.

High stakes assessment. A test in which the results will be used to determine student promotion or graduation, teacher evaluation, and/or rating of school performance.

Normed-referenced. Score is based on how a student performs in relation to other students in the tested sample, often referred to as grading "on the curve."

Readability. The level of difficulty of a particular reading passage, usually reported by a grade level.

Secure test. A testing instrument which is not available for public scrutiny, usually on the premise that someone could give out the questions and/or answers to those taking the test.

Valid assessment. A testing device that actually measures what it claims to measure (e.g., a multiplication test would include multiplication problems, not subtraction problems).

COLLABORATIVE (CO-OPERATIVE) LEARNING. Learning together not only by working in peer groups, but with businesses, health-care facilities, and other community agencies. Collaborative learning prepares students to participate in a global society. Gifted students assist their peers. Tolerance and unity are essential in achieving shared goals.

CONSENSUS. A process in which educators and citizens cooperate to forge new goals and outcomes in education. Used in such contexts as strategic planning, it may entail imposing a prearranged agenda instead of accounting for the views of each participant.

CRITICAL THINKING. Challenging fixed beliefs, traditional values, and objective truth. Instead of using reason to examine/analyze/consider the past (enabling students to think for themselves), the school's primary task is to break down old ideas, simply because they are old, and replace them with new paradigms or models because they are modern.

GLOBAL EDUCATION. Replacing traditional Western perspectives with non-Western culture and values.

MULTICULTURALISM. Appreciation and study of cultures different from one's own. Requires an openness to different belief systems and a denial that some cultures are better than others.

OBE. Education based on outcomes instead of time spent in class in specific disciplines. OBE focuses on skills that a student demonstrates rather than a body of knowledge that a student learns.

Traditional OBE. Taking existing non-OBE curriculum content and structure and adapting it so that a student's actual performance or outcomes takes precedence over time spent in class or content learned.

Transitional OBE. Moves beyond traditional OBE, as subject matter and factual recall are superseded by interdisciplinary courses that increasingly focus on what students can demonstrate by meeting carefully devised exit outcomes.

Transformational OBE. Final stage of OBE, which radically changes the entire education system.

PORTFOLIO. An assessment tool that involves collecting samples of a student's work, such as essays, projects, journals, works of art.

RUBRIC. A scoring technique that assigns a numeric value (1–4, 1–6) to levels of a child's performance, based on the subjective evaluation of one or more evaluators.

SITE-BASED MANAGEMENT. Turning over the control of schools to teams of teachers and parents who exercise authority over daily activities. Practically, this process lessens the influence of the local school board.

TRADITIONAL EDUCATION. Education based on content mastered in various disciplines. Students satisfy a distribution requirement that mandates a certain number of hours in such subjects as math, English, social studies.

WORLD-CLASS STANDARDS. Adopting ideas, methods, and competencies that will enable American students to compete favorably in a fast-changing, global environment. These tangible "standards" or outcomes have not yet been seen.

Order These Huntington House Books !

_____	America Betrayed—Marlin Maddoux	6.99 _____
_____	The Assault—Dale A. Berryhill	9.99 _____
_____	Beyond Political Correctness—David Thibodaux	9.99 _____
_____	The Best of HUMAN EVENTS—Edited by James C. Roberts	34.95 _____
_____	Can Families Survive in Pagan America?—Samuel Dresner	15.99/31.99 _____
_____	Combat Ready—Lynn Stanley	9.99 _____
_____	Conservative, American & Jewish—Jacob Neusner	9.99 _____
_____	The Dark Side of Freemasonry—Ed Decker	9.99 _____
_____	Don't Touch That Dial—Barbara Hattemer & Robert Showers	9.99/19.99 _____
_____	En Route to Global Occupation—Gary Kah	9.99 _____
_____	*Exposing the AIDS Scandal—Dr. Paul Cameron	7.99/2.99 _____
_____	The Extermination of Christianity—Paul Schenck	9.99 _____
_____	Freud's War with God—Jack Wright, Jr.	7.99 _____
_____	Goddess Earth—Samantha Smith	9.99 _____
_____	Gays & Guns—John Eidsmoe	7.99/14.99 _____
_____	Heresy Hunters—Jim Spencer	8.99 _____
_____	Hidden Dangers of the Rainbow—Constance Cumbey	9.99 _____
_____	Homeless in America—Jeremy Reynalds	9.99 _____
_____	How to Homeschool (Yes, You!)—Julia Toto	4.99 _____
_____	Hungry for God—Larry E. Myers	9.99 _____
_____	*Inside the New Age Nightmare—Randall Baer	9.99/2.99 _____
_____	A Jewish Conservative Looks at Pagan America—Don Feder	9.99/19.99 _____
_____	Journey into Darkness—Stephen Arrington	9.99 _____
_____	Kinsey, Sex and Fraud—Dr. Judith A. Reisman &	11.99 _____
	Edward Eichel (Hard cover)	
_____	The Liberal Contradiction—Dale A. Berryhill	9.99 _____
_____	Legalized Gambling—John Eidsmoe	7.99 _____
_____	Loyal Opposition—John Eidsmoe	8.99 _____
_____	The Media Hates Conservatives—Dale A. Berryhill	9.99 _____
_____	New Gods for a New Age—Richmond Odom	9.99 _____
_____	One Man, One Woman, One Lifetime—Rabbi Reuven Bulka	7.99 _____
_____	Out of Control—Brenda Scott	9.99 _____
_____	The Parched Soul of America—Leslie Kay Hedger	10.99 _____
_____	Please Tell Me—Tom McKenney	9.99 _____
_____	Political Correctness—David Thibodaux	9.99 _____
_____	Resurrecting the Third Reich—Richard Terrell	9.99 _____
_____	Revival: Its Principles and Personalities—Winkie Pratney	10.99 _____
_____	Trojan Horse—Brenda Scott & Samantha Smith	9.99 _____
_____	The Walking Wounded—Jeremy Reynalds	9.99 _____

*Available in Salt Series

Shipping & Handling _____

TOTAL _____

AVAILABLE AT BOOKSTORES EVERYWHERE or order direct from:
Huntington House Publishers•P.O. Box 53788•Lafayette, LA 70505
Send check/money order. For faster service use VISA/MASTERCARD
Call toll-free 1-800-749-4009.
Add: Freight and handling, $3.50 for the first book ordered, and $.50 for
each additional book up to 5 books.

Enclosed is $_____including postage.

VISA/MASTERCARD #_____ Exp. Date _____

Name_____ Phone: ( ) _____

Address_____

City, State, Zip_____